HISTORICAL ATLAS OF ALABAMA

Published in honor of the American Revolution
Bicentennial, 1776-1976, under the auspices
of the Alabama Bicentennial Commission.

HISTORICAL ATLAS OF ALABAMA

by
Donald B. Dodd

Cartography by
Borden D. Dent

THE UNIVERSITY OF ALABAMA PRESS
University, Alabama

917.761
D66h
96805
april 1976

Contents

Author's Preface

CENTRAL to the historian's work is the task of perceiving the elements of order in the chaotic record of human events so as to understand how the present—which is really the immediate past—developed out of the more remote past. For a similar purpose, geographers frequently use maps to illustrate the spatial distribution of a phenomenon (e.g., cotton, 1970) and, to show its development to the present, map its earlier distributions (e.g., cotton, 1860, 1900, and 1930). Geographers also use maps of other phenomena for comparative purposes (e.g., black population 1860 compared to cotton 1860).

Historical Atlas of Alabama utilizes both the comparative and changing-distribution cartographic techniques, although some unsystematic maps (e.g., Creek War maps) are used in the traditional historical way. The focal points in time are: 1860, 1900, 1930, and 1970; however, some other years are represented to show the possible effect of war or depression (1870, 1910, and 1920, 1940 1950). In some cases the expected influence of war or depression was negligible whereas a seemingly less significant factor was apparently of great moment. An example is the effect of the boll weevil on cotton production.

The topics mapped for comparison are: total population, black population, cotton, industry, education, personal wealth, and transportation. The topical maps are arranged chronologically (1900 cotton with 1900 black population) for each era covered in the *Historical Atlas* and are arranged topically (1900 cotton with 1860, 1930, and 1970 cotton) in the concluding chapter.

The narrative introductions to each chapter are designed to summarize the era, synthesize the basic patterns of the maps of the chapter, and integrate the *Atlas*. They do not exhaust the possible trends one could ascertain by comparisons to the same distributions in earlier and later years nor possible evidences of a causal relationship based on similar distributions for a different phenomenon in the same year.

It is hoped that use of the *Atlas* will enable students of Alabama history to detect central themes and to appreciate the need for some degree of quantification in the formulation of such themes. Additionally, the accurate identification of historical trends which explain the present can furnish a body of evidence for a projection of future occurrences. The emphasis of the *Historical Atlas,* however, in contrast to the recently published *Atlas of Alabama*, is on the past and the context or setting of the present rather than the present itself or the future.

It is anticipated that the *Atlas* will be of use in Alabama history courses in high school and college, and much of its organization and content is geared to that end. It should also serve as a basic reference source and point of departure for future regional studies as does *Historical Statistics of the South*.

Broad historical phenomena observable from the maps include: Alabama's physical diversity, suggesting "many Alabamas" rather than one homogeneous state; a pre-statehood role as a buffer between French and English, Spanish and English, Spanish and American and, as an American territory, between Indians and Americans; political sectionalism between "South Alabama" and "North Alabama," particularly during the secession crisis and, in the 20th Century, between the forces of conservatism ("Bourbons") and reform (Populists, Progressives, New Dealers, etc.); a history of gradual progress in education but at a rate of increase consistently less than that of the United State as a whole; and a 20th Century transition from a rural agricultural state to an urban industrial state and accompanying intrastate changes such as the Black Belt shift from a cotton-slave-plantation antebellum economy to a more diversified agricultural economy; the shift of the cotton-producing center of Alabama to the Tennessee Valley, and the Valley's change from a second class cotton-slave-plantation area of pre-Civil War days to a 20th Century economy balanced between diversified agriculture and industrialization. Alabama history, as all history, has one consistent theme—the only unchanging thing in human relations is the constancy of change itself.

Most of the statistics used as a basis for the thematic maps (1860, 1900, 1930, 1970, etc.) were compiled from published reports of the

United States Bureau of the Census. State agencies which provided data for their subject areas include: Alabama Department of Aeronautics, Alabama State Planning and Development Board, the Secretary of State's Office, and the State Department of Conservation. The Alabama State Department of Archives and History was particularly helpful with special assistance being given the author by Jessie Cobb, Frances Clark, Virginia Jones, and the late Bill Letford. Sara Elizabeth Mason of the Birmingham Public Library coordinated the use of the Rucker Agee Collection (particularly concerning the European period and the Creek Indian War materials). The Black Voter map is based on Southern Regional Council data, the Alabama Authors list on Ben Williams' *Literary History of Alabama,* and the trend charts following Chapter XII on Alabama data from *Historical Statistics of the South.*

A special boost to the *Historical Atlas* project came with the addition of Professor Borden Dent and his team of student cartographers at Georgia State University. The high quality of their work is exceeded only by their cooperation in fulfilling the technical needs of the project. Especially helpful to Professor Dent were Eugene Loring, who played a significant part in the ultimate design of the maps and worked with much of the material leading to the final maps; several of Professor Dent's cartography students, who did most of the work of assembling the various parts of the maps; and the support given the project by Professor Dent's parent institution, Georgia State University.

The author is also grateful for the encouragement in the fields of Southern history and geography provided by his former graduate school teachers: Malcolm McMillan, Frank L. Owsley, Jr., and Tom Belser of Auburn University and Charles E. Wynes and the late Rembert W. Patrick of the University of Georgia, who tutored him in Alabama and Southern history; and Merle Prunty, Louis DeVorsey, James Barnes, and Gerald Holder of the University of Georgia Geography Department, who taught him to appreciate the value of maps in historical work.

The project was supported by a grant from Auburn University at Montgomery, which provided able typing assistance from Mrs. Macalyn Boyles and Mrs. Cathy Crockett and secretarial assistance from Mrs. Hildreth Heinen, Mrs. Marilee Mallory, and Miss Jennie Farmer. Dr. Morgan Walters, Mr. Jim Travis, and Mr. Paul Kennedy of the University of Alabama Press encouraged and supported the project throughout. The author is also grateful for the encouragement given the project through research, drafting of early rough maps, and typing by his wife Sandra Whitten Dodd, and by "kid help" from our two children, Donna and Brad, who seem to understand the long hours away from home on this and other projects.

Cartographer's Preface

OFTEN the size or scale of a printed map will determine the kind of design judgments that lead to its final rendering. The maps in this volume are a good example of this. The fundamental problem was to present maps with considerable necessary detail, yet keep their lettering and symbols at a size that is easily readable. We believe an acceptable balance has been struck in this regard. To overcome this crowding problem we were forced to use more maps, with singular information on each. This approach has merit, however, in that the message on each map is quite clear, and there is little possibility of reading error.

A note should be conveyed regarding the unusual way in which the shape of the state and its counties is portrayed. The reader will see that all boundaries have been somewhat adjusted, making them into straight segments. One may first react by saying this is not truthful mapping, as we know that many of these boundaries are irregularly curved ones (as in the case of a river boundary at our scale). The rationale adopted was that the *exact* geographic location of the boundaries is not of paramount importance. What is critical is that the *general distribution qualities* of the items being mapped should be clear, concise, and meaningful. To this end, the adjusted boundaries prove quite adequate, with little detail at our scale actually being lost.

Many of the maps in the volume are thematic illustrations—maps portraying one theme or geographic distribution. The maps showing cotton production are examples of this kind. A proportional point symbol was chosen to visually depict the data. For these maps, the data for all the counties were first classed into meaningful groups, and then circles were drawn in each county proportional to the mid-points of the class in which the county values belonged. As map readers tend to underestimate the area beneath these symbols, and hence relative size comparisons are made difficult, they were adjusted to compensate for this visual tendency. For all similar maps throughout the project, computer programs were utilized to do the onerous calculation tasks involving data arraying and circle size computation.

On those maps that illustrate one theme over a period of years, for example the several different population maps, the classes are identical from year to year wherever possible. This facilitates not only our depicting relative pictures of these distributions, but absolute ones as well.

The maps of mean annual temperature, precipitation, and growing season days may be unfamiliar to the map reader. To understand these maps one should mentally form a three-dimensional, undulating surface above the state, with various high and low points. This surface can be likened to a rubber sheet stretched over several pins, each pin having a height proportional to the value represented in each county. The lines on these maps represent the contact between a hypothetical plane at some value height with this undulating surface and, as a result, along each line we find an identical value. These kinds of maps are to be taken quite *generally,* their great service being in their ability to convey simply the overall character of a geographic distribution.

The political maps use a somewhat different symbolization scheme. In these cases the entire area of a county is rendered in a printed color, and the greater the amount represented, the darker the color-value. These kinds of maps are called choropleth maps and are quite common cartographic illustrations. The one assumption that is made for these maps is that the value represented in a county is thought to be evenly distributed throughout the county unit. These maps, like the ones using proportional circles, impart a feeling for the overall distribution of the mapped values.

One of the great values to the reader of this volume is its capability of conveying a sense of the temporal changes throughout the period covered. The reader is alerted to this capability and he should use the maps whenever possible. Maps that can be used in this way have been placed on opposite facing pages to facilitate comparisons. Relative and absolute increases and decreases can then be observed quite easily. Having a collection of maps that reflect temporal changes for many of the important elements in the historical development of the state sets this volume apart. Far too often, maps are presented without this time dimension. It is the presence of the time dimension that makes many of the maps herein exceptionally relevant to the reader.

HISTORICAL ATLAS OF ALABAMA

Chapter One

*The Land Called Alabama**

ALABAMA is named for the Alabama River which, in turn, received its namesake from the Alabamas, an Indian tribe which once lived near the present site of Montgomery. "Alabama" is a Choctaw word meaning "thicket clearers" or "vegetation gatherers."

The State lies between 84°51' and 88°31' west longitude and 30°13' and 35° north latitude. Its greatest length is 335 miles and greatest width 220 miles. Its area is 51,609 square miles.

Alabama's resources include a network of navigable rivers, a temperate climate, generally fertile soil, many minerals, and extensive forests. The Tennessee River, flowing westward for 200 miles from the northeastern corner of the state to the northwestern corner, is now navigable for its entire length, as is the Tombigbee, north to Columbus, Mississippi; the Warrior, to Birmingham Port; the Alabama, to Wetumpka; and the Chattahoochee, to Columbus, Georgia. The fertile river valleys were centers of Indian and later European civilizations, and the waterways were main transportation routes prior to railroads and paved roads. The temperature (60° mean in north to 67° in south), the precipitation (52'' to 68'' mean annual), the length of the growing season (198 days in the north to 298 in the south), the elevation (600 feet mean for the State, 800 feet for the highlands), the arrangement of the highlands, the proximity to the Gulf, and the prevailing winds all contribute to a temperate and uniform climate. This climate, interacting with the natural vegetation and an adequate drainage system, has produced generally fertile soils, and contributes to the State's having been predominantly agricultural

*From Malcolm McMillan, *The Land Called Alabama* (Austin, Texas: Steck-Vaughn Co., 1969)—the most comprehensive survey of the State in print.

for much of its history. The current agricultural areas (based on the crops which yield the highest dollar value in the respective areas) vary due to the relative emphasis given to the predominant crops of cotton, corn, soybeans, wheat, and peanuts. The land under the soil is likewise productive; a significant part of the total labor force of several Alabama counties is engaged in mining, particularly in the area of northwest Alabama within a radius of 75 miles from Walker County.

Considered as a group, these geographic characteristics suggest a homogeneous State. In actuality, there are "many Alabamas" from a physical standpoint, with each of the five physiographic provinces significantly different. The Highland Rim in the northwest is more like central Tennessee to the north than other physical areas of the state and contains the Tennessee Valley which, through TVA, has helped make Alabama fifth in the nation in hydroelectric plants and Huntsville "the Rocket City." The Cumberland Plateau shares a hilly or mountainous terrain with the Appalachian Highlands, which extend north to central New York. The Ridge and Valley, an area of sandstone ridges and limestone valleys, parallels the Plateau north-easterly to the Great Valley of the Shenandoah, and the Alabama portion contains three of Alabama's most important coal and iron centers—Birmingham, Gadsden, and Anniston. The Piedmont, an erosional plain with a few hills rising above its otherwise gently rolling surface, shares a "mineral belt" classification with the Ridge and Valley area and a hydroelectric capacity with the Highland Rim through projects on the Tallapoosa, Coosa, and Chattahoochee rivers. The Coastal Plain, covering two-thirds of the state, has been, historically, both a "Timber Belt" and an agricultural area and includes the "Black Belt"—the center of the cotton-slave-plantation economy of antebellum Alabama.

ALABAMA IN A REGIONAL SETTING 1970
SHOWING CITIES AND TOWNS
WITH GREATER THAN 25,000 POPULATION

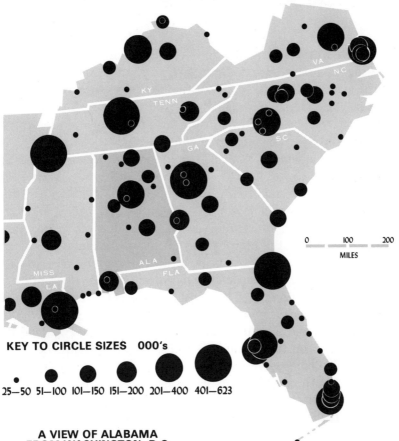

0   100   200
MILES

KEY TO CIRCLE SIZES   000's

25—50 51—100 101—150 151—200 201—400 401—623

A VIEW OF ALABAMA
FROM WASHINGTON, D.C.

1970 TOTAL STATE POPULATIONS

FLORIDA	6,789,000
NORTH CAROLINA	5,082,000
VIRGINIA	4,648,000
GEORGIA	4,590,000
TENNESSEE	3,924,000
LOUISIANA	3,641,000
ALABAMA	3,444,000
KENTUCKY	3,219,000
SOUTH CAROLINA	2,591,000
MISSISSIPPI	2,217,000

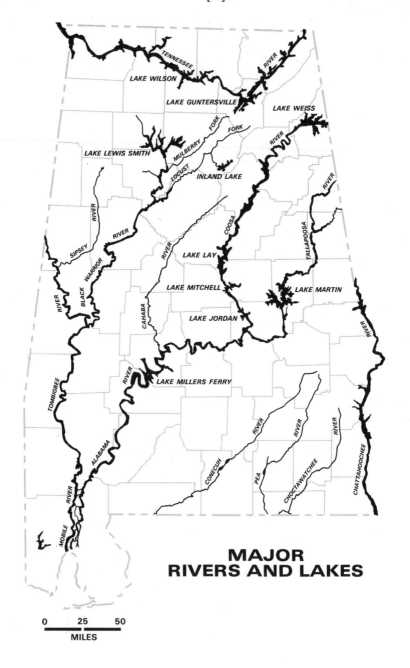

**MAJOR
RIVERS AND LAKES**

0   25   50
MILES

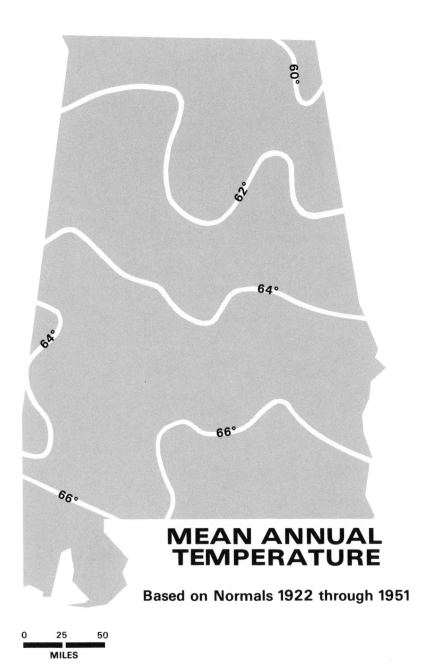

MEAN ANNUAL TEMPERATURE

Based on Normals 1922 through 1951

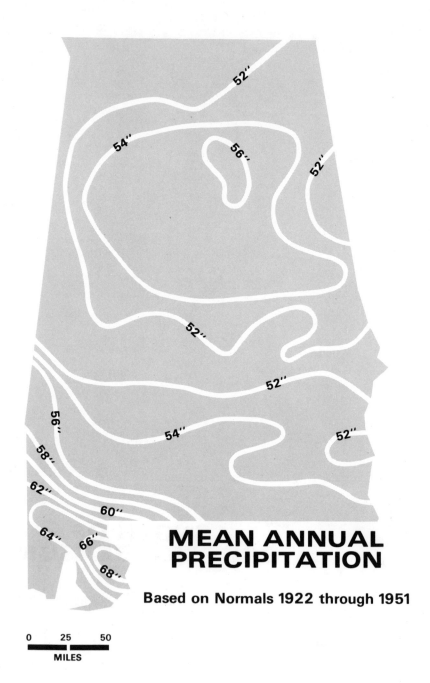

MEAN ANNUAL PRECIPITATION

Based on Normals 1922 through 1951

0   25   50
MILES

LENGTH OF GROWING SEASON

DAYS

0   25   50
MILES

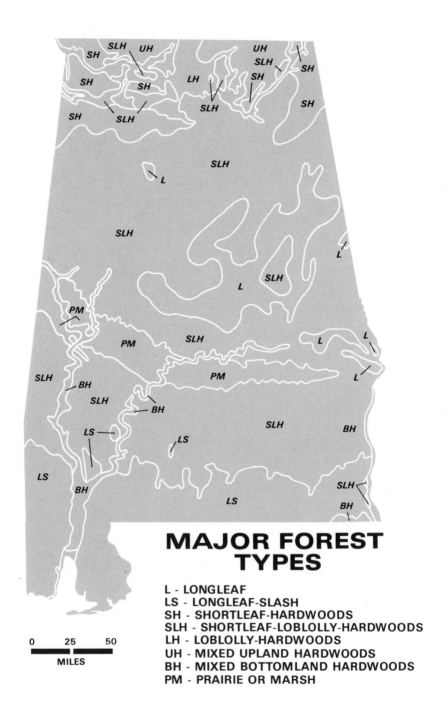

MAJOR FOREST TYPES

L - LONGLEAF
LS - LONGLEAF-SLASH
SH - SHORTLEAF-HARDWOODS
SLH - SHORTLEAF-LOBLOLLY-HARDWOODS
LH - LOBLOLLY-HARDWOODS
UH - MIXED UPLAND HARDWOODS
BH - MIXED BOTTOMLAND HARDWOODS
PM - PRAIRIE OR MARSH

0   25   50
MILES

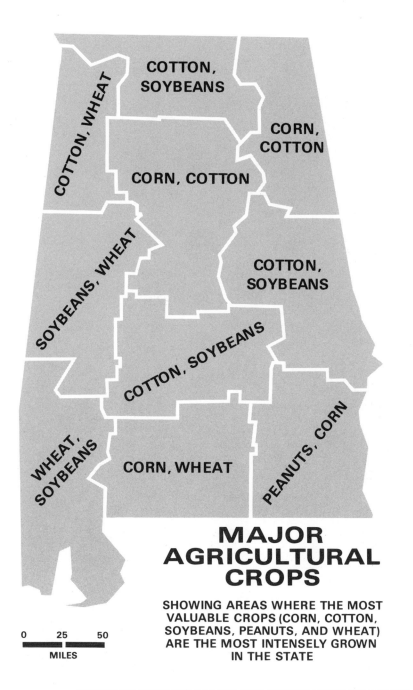

COTTON, WHEAT

COTTON, SOYBEANS

CORN, COTTON

CORN, COTTON

SOYBEANS, WHEAT

COTTON, SOYBEANS

COTTON, SOYBEANS

WHEAT, SOYBEANS

CORN, WHEAT

PEANUTS, CORN

MAJOR AGRICULTURAL CROPS

SHOWING AREAS WHERE THE MOST VALUABLE CROPS (CORN, COTTON, SOYBEANS, PEANUTS, AND WHEAT) ARE THE MOST INTENSELY GROWN IN THE STATE

0   25   50

MILES

BOUNDARIES REPRESENT THE TEN AGRICULTURAL REPORTING REGIONS

EMPLOYMENT IN MINING 1970

PERCENT OF TOTAL EMPLOYMENT

0   25   50
MILES

0-.90   .91-1.50   1.51-4.50   4.51-9.00

HIGHLAND RIM

PLATEAU

RIDGE AND
VALLEY

PIEDMONT

BLACK BELT

COASTAL PLAINS

PHYSIOGRAPHIC
REGIONS

0   25   50

MILES

Chapter Two

Under Five Flags:
Europeans Invade Alabama

THE five flags over Alabama were the French (1702-1763), the British (1763-1780), the Spanish (1780-1813), the United States (1813-1861; 1865-present), and the Confederate (1861-1865). The Spanish were the first to explore the coast and interior of Alabama, but the French made the first permanent settlement.

Although the Alabama coastline was accurately portrayed on European maps as early as 1507, the first known Spanish explorer of the Alabama coast was Alonzo de Piñeda, who entered Mobile Bay in 1519. Piñeda was followed by Panfilo de Narváez (1528), Hernando de Soto (1540), Guido de las Bazáres (1558), and Tristan de Luna (1559-1561). The most thorough exploration was by de Soto in 1540.

Hernando do Soto, a veteran of the Pizarro expedition to Peru, arrived at Tampa Bay in May, 1539. Approximately four years later, the one-half of the expedition which survived arrived in Mexico. In the four years, the Spanish explored Florida, Georgia, parts of the Carolinas and Tennessee, Alabama, Mississippi, Louisiana, Arkansas, and Texas.

The first permanent settlement in Alabama was made by the French at Mobile in 1702, by the Le Moyne brothers, Iberville and Bienville. The first site of Mobile was at Twenty-Seven Mile Bluff and was named "Fort Louis de la Mobile" for Louis XIV and nearby Indians. Fort Louis was moved to the present site of Mobile in 1711 and was replaced, in 1717, by an extensive brick fortress called Fort Conde. During their tenure, the French built Fort Tombeckbee on the Tombigbee River as a base against the pro-English Chickasaws, and Fort Toulouse at the confluence of the Coosa and Tallapoosa rivers near present day Wetumpka. The latter fort was established as a trading post, a military outpost against the British, and a bar to communication and trade between the British on the Atlantic coast and the Chickasaws to the west. The British countered the Fort Toulouse move by establishing Fort Okfuski shortly after the founding of Georgia in 1733. The Treaty of Paris (1763) ending the French and Indian War ceded all of French Louisiana east of New Orleans to England, including the French forts in Alabama.

The British took over Mobile on October 20, 1763. Fort Conde was renamed Fort Charlotte in honor of the reigning British queen, wife of George III. Fort Tombeckbee was renamed Fort York. The former French forts were allowed to deteriorate, however, and in March, 1780, Bernardo Galvez, the young Governor of Louisiana, captured Mobile with ease. Galvez's gains were consolidated in the Treaty of Paris (1783), which ceded Florida to Spain.

The early Spanish occupation after the Revolution was marked by a boundary conflict with the Americans. The Spanish claimed the area north to 32° 28' and the Americans claimed the land south to 31° (south of the Spanish Fort of St. Stephens). Spain accepted the American claim in Pinckney's Treaty of 1795, and in 1798 the Americans occupied St. Stephens.

The Spanish era was marked by US-Spanish competition for trade and allies among the Southern Indians. Spanish-supplied Indians attacked American frontier settlements, and the rivalry spilled over into the Creek Indian War, 1813-1814. Young America, however, became too much for distant Spain. Mobile fell to the Americans in 1813 during the War of 1812 and within a decade the area was ceded to the US by the Adams-Oñis Treaty.

HERNANDO DESOTO'S EXPEDITION IN THE SOUTHEAST 1540

Ft. Atassi (1730)

Ft. Okfuski (1735)

Ft. Tombeckbee (1735)

Ft. Toulouse (1715)

Ft. Louis (1702)

FRENCH IN ALABAMA
1670-1763

Ft. Conde (1711)

0   25   50

MILES

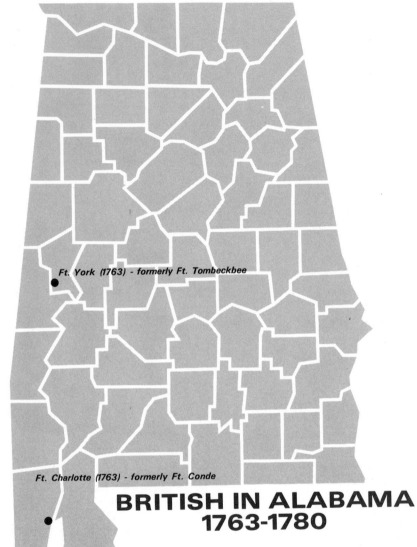

Ft. York (1763) - formerly Ft. Tombeckbee

Ft. Charlotte (1763) - formerly Ft. Conde

BRITISH IN ALABAMA
1763-1780

0   25   50

MILES

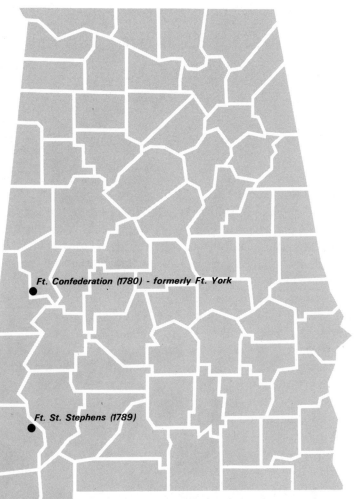

Ft. Confederation (1780) - formerly Ft. York

Ft. St. Stephens (1789)

Spanish Fort (1780)

Ft. Serof (1803)

SPANISH IN ALABAMA
1780-1813

0   25   50

MILES

Chapter Three

The Creek Indian War
1813-1814

THE westward movement into Alabama and British and Spanish intrigue led to the Creek Indian War, 1813-1814. American settlers expanded the "bridle paths" through the Creek Nation to major highways of migration and the Creeks faced the prospect of being hemmed in between Georgians and the settlers along the Tombigbee River. British-American grievances leading into the War of 1812 influenced British agents in Canada to send the Shawnee Chief Tecumseh south for allies among the Choctaws, Chickasaws, Cherokees, Seminoles, and Creeks. Tecumseh's oratory was effectively countered by the Choctaw Chief Pushmataha among the Choctaws and Chickasaws, but a war party of "Red Sticks" (Creek symbol of war) developed among the Creeks.

The Alabama settlers followed the Indian developments closely and, when it was learned a "Red Stick" force was securing arms in Spanish Florida, a body of Mississippi Territory militiamen attacked the returning party in a bend of Burnt Corn Creek. After an initial success, the militia became occupied with spoils and were routed by a Red Stick counterattack.

Terrified by the Red Stick success at Burnt Corn Creek, the Alabama pioneers left their cabins for refuge in the nearest frontier fort. Five hundred fifty-three settlers, including approximately 100 children and 175 soldiers, gathered at Fort Mims, a hastily erected one-acre stockade around the home of Samuel Mims near Lake Tensas north of Mobile. On August 30, 1813, more than 1,000 Red Sticks attacked the fort and killed most of its occupants.

The loss of Fort Mims alarmed neighboring areas and expeditions against the Red Sticks were soon launched from Tennessee, Mississippi, and Georgia. General Andrew Jackson led his "Tennessee Volunteers" south and, aided by friendly Chickasaws, Cherokees and some Creeks, had victories at Talladega, Tallasehatche, and Enita-chopco, and a stalemate at Emuckfau. General F. J. Claiborne led his Mississippi militiamen north and, assisted by Choctaws under Push-mataha, defeated a Red Stick party under William Weatherford ("Red Eagle") at Holy Ground. Short enlistments forced Claiborne to withdraw to a more fortified position shortly after his victory. General John Floyd moved west from Fort Mitchell, near the Georgia line, and was defeated by the Red Sticks at Calabee Creek. With the retirement of Claiborne and Floyd, the Creek War was left to Jackson.

In February, 1814, Jackson, at his Fort Strother base, learned of a Red Stick concentration in the bend of the Tallapoosa River—"Horseshoe Bend." At the Horseshoe, Jackson and his 2,000 militia-men found about 1,000 Red Sticks under Menowa entrenched behind breastworks in the "open end" of the Horseshoe with the river on three sides. Jackson sent General John Coffee across the river to cut off the anticipated Red Stick retreat and led his main column against the breastworks. Some of Coffee's men swam the Tallapoosa River, destroyed Red Stick canoes, and burned the village of Tohopeka in the rear of the Red Sticks at about the same time that Jackson's men launched their attack. Although Menowa escaped and some women and children were captured, almost 1,000 Red Sticks were killed.

The Battle of the Horseshoe broke the back of the Red Stick rebellion and opened the entire Southwest to American settlers. The Creeks surrendered about one-half of the present state of Alabama in August, 1814, at Fort Jackson. By the time Alabama became a state in 1819, at least three-fourths of the state had been ceded by the Indians, including land owned by the friendly Choctaws, Chickasaws, and Cherokees. By a series of treaties between 1828 and 1835, the remaining Indian land was ceded.

Ft. Easley
Ft. Mott
Ft. Turner
Ft. White
Ft. Cato
Ft. Sinquefield
Ft. McGrew
Ft. Landrum
Ft. Madison
Ft. Republic
Ft. Glass
Ft. Carney
Ft. Claiborne
Ft. Curry
Ft. Mims
Ft. Rankin
Ft. Pierce
Ft. Deposit

CREEK INDIAN WARS
1813-1814
PHASE OF WAR OF 1812

● Lower Tombigbee Settlements

o Forts Built by Gen. F. L. Claiborne's
 Mississippians

All forts established in 1813 except Ft. Mims (1812)

0   25   50

MILES

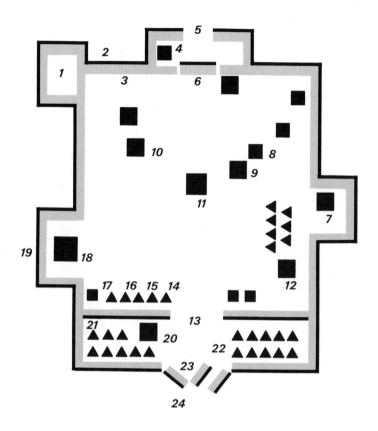

FORT MIMS

1 Block House
2 Pickets cut away by the Indians
3 Guard's Station
4 Guard House
5 Western Gate, but not up
6 This gate was shut, but a hole
   was cut through by the Indians
7 Captain Bailey's Station
8 Steadham's House
9 Mrs. Dyer's House
10 Kitchen
11 Mim's House
12 Randon's House
13 Old Gate-way-open
14 Ensign Chambliss's Tent
15 Ensign Gibbs'
16 Randon's
17 Captain Middleton's
18 Captain Jack's Station
19 Port-holes taken by Indians
20 Major Beasley's Cabin
21 Captain Jack's Company
22 Captain Middleton's Company
23 Where Major Beasley fell
24 Eastern Gate
   Where the Indians entered

FORT HAMPTON

TENNESSEE

Huntsville

Tennessee River

FORT DEPOSIT

Route of Gen. Jackson's Army to the Creek Nation

Route of Gen. Cock's Army

MISSISSIPPI TERRITORY

FORT STROTHER

FORT ARMSTRONG

Part of Gen. Cock's Army joined Jackson's Army by this route

CREEK INDIAN WAR

Talladega

UPPER CREEKS

■ FORT
• Indian Settlements
● Principal Towns

River

GEORGIA

0 10 20 30
miles

Coosee

Tallapoosee

River

Tuskegee

Road from New Orleans

River

Coweta

Chatahouchy River

LOWER CREEKS

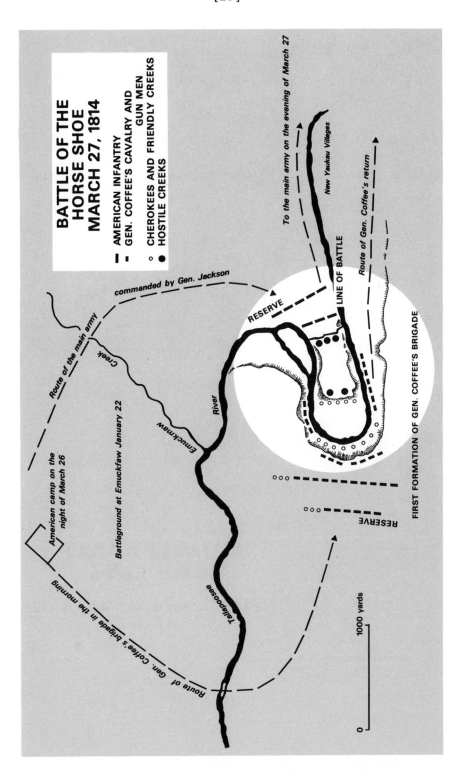

BATTLE OF THE
HORSE SHOE
MARCH 27, 1814

AMERICAN INFANTRY
GEN. COFFEE'S CAVALRY AND
GUN MEN
CHEROKEES AND FRIENDLY CREEKS
HOSTILE CREEKS

commanded by Gen. Jackson

Route of the main army

American camp on the
night of March 26

Creek

Battleground at Emuckfaw January 22

Emuckfaw

River

Route of Gen. Coffee's brigade in the morning

Tallapoosee

RESERVE

LINE OF BATTLE

RESERVE

To the main army on the evening of March 27

New Yaukau Villages

Route of Gen. Coffee's return

FIRST FORMATION OF GEN. COFFEE'S BRIGADE

0   1000 yards

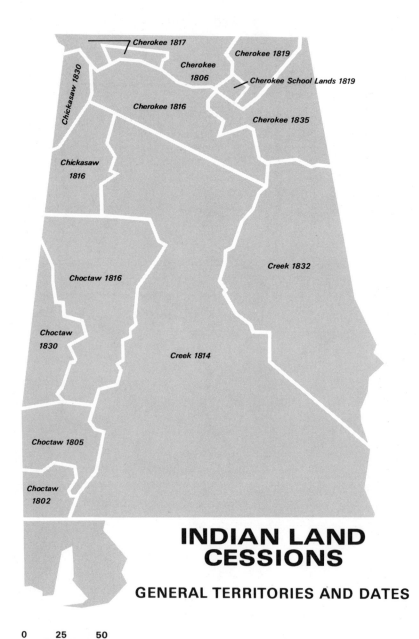

Cherokee 1817

Cherokee 1819

Chickasaw 1830

Cherokee
1806

Cherokee School Lands 1819

Cherokee 1816

Cherokee 1835

Chickasaw
1816

Creek 1832

Choctaw 1816

Choctaw
1830

Creek 1814

Choctaw 1805

Choctaw
1802

INDIAN LAND
CESSIONS

GENERAL TERRITORIES AND DATES

0   25   50

MILES

Chapter Four

Territorial Changes in Alabama
1798-1974

THE Mississippi territory as created by the 1798 act of Congress included all the territory now in Alabama and Mississippi north of 31° and south of 32° 28'. The 1802 cession of Georgia's western lands to the U.S. added the land now in Alabama and Mississippi which is north of 32° 28'. The War of 1812 conquest of Mobile completed the limits of the present state.

The territorial and statehood status of Alabama was determined by the provisions of the Northwest Ordinance of 1787. When Mississippi was admitted as a state in 1817, the Alabama Territory was created and two years later Alabama became a state.

St. Stephens (present Washington County) was the territorial capital. Since statehood, the State Capitals have been Huntsville (1819-1820), Cahaba in Dallas County (1820-1826), Tuscaloosa (1826-1846), and Montgomery (1846-present).

The number of counties in Alabama has increased from 30 in 1819 to 67 in 1974. The number has remained constant since Houston became the 67th county in 1903. Indian cessions, population growth, and political developments have contributed to the changes in county boundaries noted in the county outline maps in this chapter.

With county boundary changes, changing county "centers," and populations shifts, have come changes in county seats. County seat changes in the last century can be noted by comparing the 1872 and 1972 county seat maps. For example, the county seat towns of Frankfort, Somerville, Pikeville, Houston, Lebanon, Elyton, Linden, Seale, Rutledge, Pollard, St. Stephens, and Blakely have been replaced by Russellville, Decatur, Hamilton, Double Springs, Ft. Payne, Birmingham, Demopolis, Phenix City, Luverne, Brewton, Chatom, and Bay Minette.

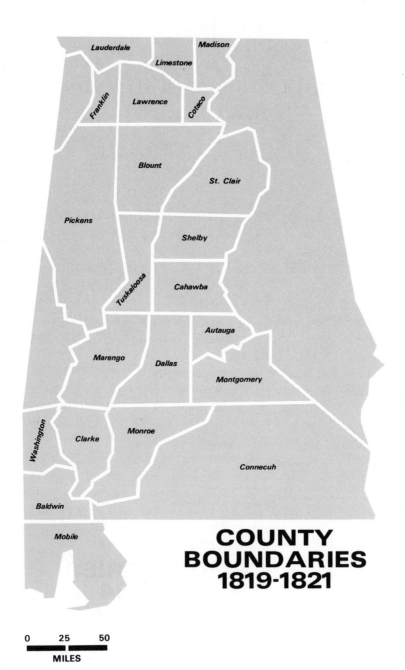

COUNTY BOUNDARIES 1819-1821

0   25   50
MILES

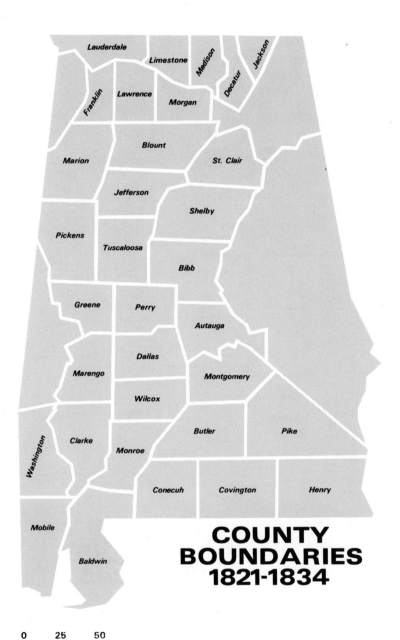

COUNTY BOUNDARIES 1821-1834

0   25   50
MILES

COUNTY BOUNDARIES 1834-1845

0   25   50
MILES

COUNTY BOUNDARIES 1845-1852

0   25   50
MILES

COUNTY
BOUNDARIES
1860

0   25   50

MILES

COUNTY BOUNDARIES 1870

MILES

COUNTY BOUNDARIES 1880-1890

0   25   50

MILES

COUNTY BOUNDARIES 1900

0   25   50
MILES

COUNTY BOUNDARIES 1910-1972

0   25   50
MILES

COUNTY SEATS 1872

0 25 50

MILES

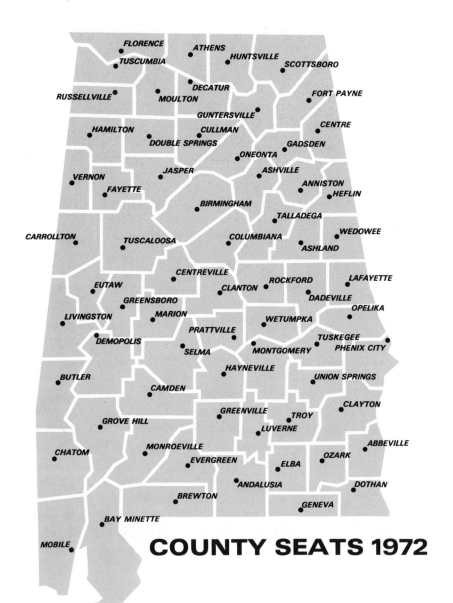

COUNTY SEATS 1972

0   25   50

MILES

Chapter Five

Antebellum Alabama

THE moving of the capital from Tuscaloosa to Montgomery in 1846 heralded the arrival of the Black Belt as the dominant section in the economic and political life of antebellum Alabama. Alabama was the "Cotton State" and the Black Belt was the center of cotton production. Cotton was king and its barons were Black Belt planters.

Cotton constituted approximately 60 percent of the total exports of the United States in 1860 and almost one-fourth of the cotton came from Alabama. Mobile received raw cotton from the plantations near the Tombigbee and Alabama rivers and ranked second only to New Orleans as the largest cotton port in the South. In fact, Alabama contributed to the premier status of the Louisiana port because the Tennessee Valley planters of north Alabama shipped their cotton via the Tennessee River north to the Ohio River and thence to and down the Mississippi to New Orleans and the Gulf of Mexico. Most of Alabama's cotton, however, was produced in the Black Belt. In 1860, the ten leading Black Belt counties produced more than the remaining forty-two counties combined.

The Black Belt was also the most densely populated part of the State, primarily because 45 percent of the State's black population was concentrated there as a part of the slave-cotton-plantation complex or the "Cotton Kingdom." Secondary areas of population density, white and black, were the Tennessee, Coosa, Tombigbee, and Alabama river valleys.

A negative concomitant of "Cotton Kingdom" prosperity was the deprivation of educational opportunity suffered by the slaves. As a consequence, Alabama's illiteracy rate in 1870 was highest in the antebellum "Cotton Kingdom" area. Although the Public School Acts of 1854 and 1856 had instituted a statewide public school system, the better public schools were in cities such as Mobile. The

"Cotton Kingdom" education blight was shared to some degree by rural areas all over the State.

The urban areas in 1860 were not notably superior in culture, however, as they were principally central collection and distribution points for the agricultural economy. They were also not large. Although the Mobile area had almost 30,000 residents, Montgomery (8,843), Tuscaloosa (3,989), and Selma (3,177) were relatively small. There was a theater at Mobile and portrait painters roamed the State but the intellectual life of antebellum Alabama cities was primarily centered around the local newspaper, of which there were almost 100 by 1860.

The antebellum industrial and transportation developments focused on the cities. The manufacturing center of the State was the Montgomery area, where Daniel Pratt had the largest cotton gin factory in the world. Alabama also ranked fourth among Southern states in textiles.

Stagecoach lines served most Alabama cities, and railroads had made some inroads by the 1850s. By 1854 the Memphis and Charleston Railroad had become an alternate means of transportation for residents of the Tennessee Valley, and Montgomery and Atlanta were connected by rail. Montgomery had a rail link to Mobile Bay by the end of the Civil War. Mobile, in turn, was the southernmost stop of the Mobile and Ohio Railroad, which ran north to Cairo, Illinois. The railroads, combined with the navigable rivers, made Alabama's transportation system one of the best in the South.

A major undeveloped area was the hill region of North Alabama, which cut the transportation and cultural link between the Tennessee Valley and South Alabama. The "Cotton Kingdom" did not extend to the hills. The disparity between the hill culture and the plantation culture was reflected in an intrastate sectionalism that resulted in bloodshed during the Civil War. The cotton-producing areas, where the most families owned slaves, supported the extension of slavery westward into the United States territories, opposed the election of Lincoln, and voted for secession delegates to the 1861 Secession Convention. In contrast, areas not in the "Cotton Kingdom" were generally not enthusiastic for slavery or secession.

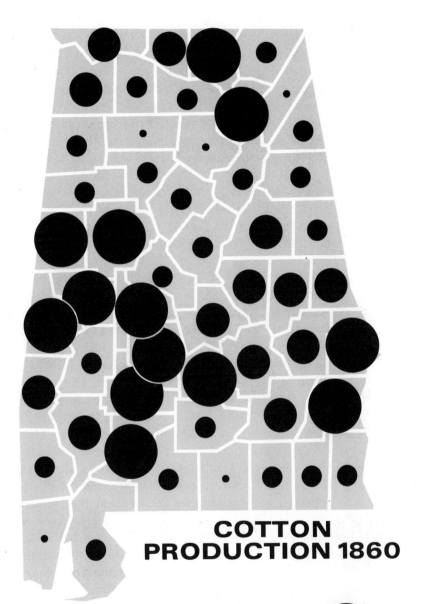

COTTON PRODUCTION 1860

BALES (x 100)

1-20   21-135   136-250   251-634

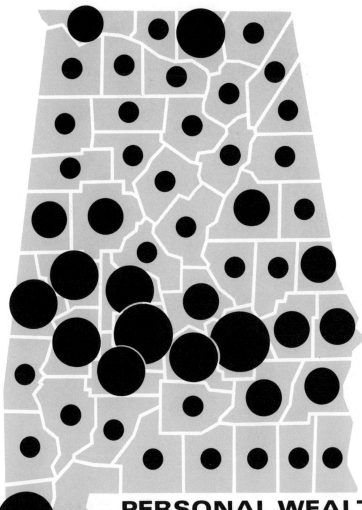

**PERSONAL WEALTH
1860**
REAL AND PERSONAL
PROPERTY VALUATION

1860 DOLLARS
(x 1,000,000)

0   25   50
MILES

.6-   13.6-   26.6-   39.6-
13.5   26.5   39.5   51.9

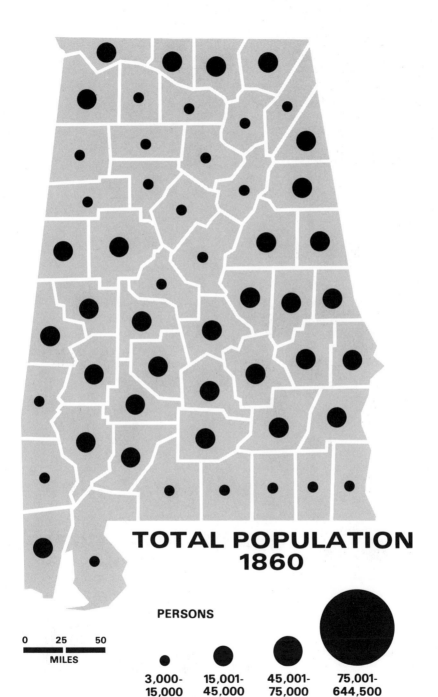

**TOTAL POPULATION
1860**

PERSONS

0   25   50
MILES

3,000-
15,000

15,001-
45,000

45,001-
75,000

75,001-
644,500

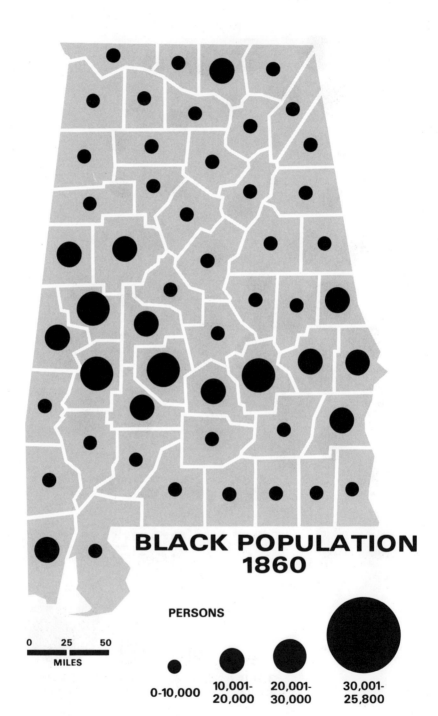

BLACK POPULATION 1860

PERSONS

0 25 50
MILES

0-10,000

10,001-
20,000

20,001-
30,000

30,001-
25,800

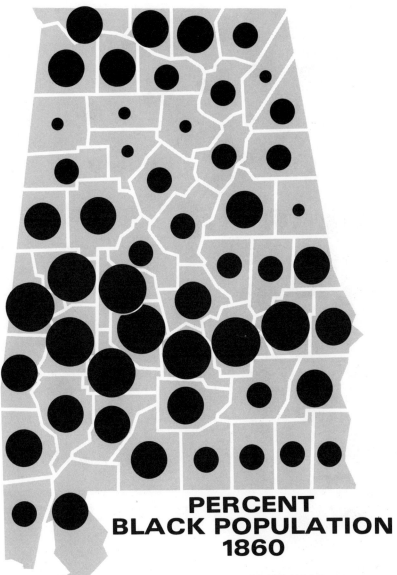

**PERCENT
BLACK POPULATION
1860**

PERCENT OF TOTAL POPULATION

MILES

0-12.0   12.1-36.0   36.1-60.0   60.1-90.0

ILLITERACY 1870

PERCENT ILLITERATE

0   25   50
MILES

5.1-12.0   12.1-24.0   24.1-36.0   36.1-52.0

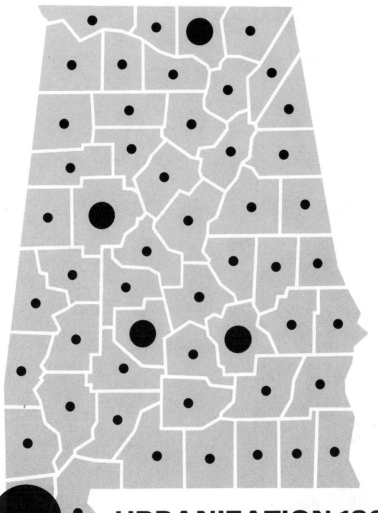

URBANIZATION 1860

**PERCENT OF TOTAL POPULATION
LIVING IN TOWNS OF 2,500 OR MORE**

0   25   50
MILES

0   0.1-30.0   30.1-60.0   60.1-90.0

INDUSTRY 1860
VALUE ADDED BY MANUFACTURING

DOLLARS

0   25   50
MILES

| 0-50,000 | 50,001-100,000 | 100,001-300,000 | 300,001-835,000 |

RAILROADS 1860

0   25   50

MILES

**SLAVE OWNERSHIP
1860**

PERCENT OF FAMILIES WHO OWN SLAVES

2-17
18-31
32-50
51-84

0   25   50
MILES

**ELECTION OF
DELEGATES TO
SECESSION
CONVENTION**

0   25   50
MILES

SECESSIONIST BY MORE THAN 70%
OF TOTAL WHITE POPULATION

SECESSIONIST 50% - 70%

ANTI-SECESSIONIST 50% TO 70%

ANTI-SECESSIONIST BY MORE THAN 70%

Chapter Six

Chapter Six

Civil War Alabama

THE Republican Abraham Lincoln won the presidential election of 1860 and, in conformance to an earlier State legislative act, Governor Andrew Barry Moore proclaimed Christmas eve, 1860, as the day when Alabamians would elect delegates to a state convention for the purpose of resolving the "crisis." The elected delegates met in Montgomery in January, 1861, and, led by South Alabama delegates, voted 54 to 46 for immediate, separate-state secession from the Union. Seven anti-immediate secessionists later switched sides to make the final vote 61 to 39.

Ironically, North Alabama, whose delegates generally opposed the convention's decision, was the section which suffered the most during the war which followed secession. Most of the conflicts between Union and Confederate forces in the years 1861-1864 occurred in the Tennessee Valley area although there were periodic Union raids into other parts of the State and considerable late war action in South Alabama, particularly with the fall of Selma and Mobile in April, 1865. The major raids were Streight's Raid (1863), Rousseau's Raid (1864), and Wilson-Croxton's Raid (1865). Streight had limited success before being defeated by Nathan B. Forrest, but the Union raids of Rousseau and Wilson-Croxton were highly successful. Rousseau accomplished his prime purpose of cutting the railroad link between Montgomery and Atlanta before joining Sherman at Atlanta, and Wilson destroyed the Confederate ordnance and manufacturing center at Selma. Croxton's raiders, a detachment from Wilson's main column, burned the University of Alabama (a training center for Confederate cadets). After the war, Congress gave the University of Alabama public lands to compensate for this wartime loss.

Alabamians participated on all fronts during the Civil War and in both armies. Approximately 67,000 to 100,000 Alabamians served in the Confederate Army and an estimated 12,500 in the Union Army (about 2,500 white and 10,000 black).

The war resulted in an impoverished Alabama. The sacrifices made to support the Confederate war effort and the ravages of both armies left much of the state (but particularly North Alabama) destitute. Manufacturing made some advances during the war and the transportation system was improved through railroads, but the Union raids late in the war canceled these modest gains.

The 1860 and 1870 maps of population and cotton indicate some other changes in the State due to the war. The Black Belt remained the leading area in both total and black population, but after the war the Tennessee Valley replaced the Piedmont as second in total population, and there was a greater concentration of blacks near Selma and Montgomery in the post-war era. The cotton distribution remained basically constant with the Black Belt and Tennessee Valley ranking first and second; however, there was a marked decrease in the amount of cotton produced all over the State.

CIVIL WAR RAIDS

GEN. JOHN CROXTON   *(Chickasaw to Georgia Line, 1865)*
GEN. JOHN GEARY   *(Blakely to Eufaula, 1865)*
GEN. BENJIMAN GRIERSON   *(Bridgeport to Triana, 1864)*
GEN. THOMAS LUCUS   *(Blakely to Montgomery, 1865)*
GEN. LOVELL ROUSSEAU   *(Decatur to Georgia Line, 1864)*
COL. ANDREW SPURLING   *(Milton, Fla. to Canoe Station, 1865)*
GEN. FREDERICK STEELE   *(Pensacola, Fla. to Blakely, 1865)*
COL. ABEL STREIGHT   *(Chickasaw to Cedar Bluff, 1863)*
GEN. JAMES WILSON   *(Chickasaw to Girard, 1865)*

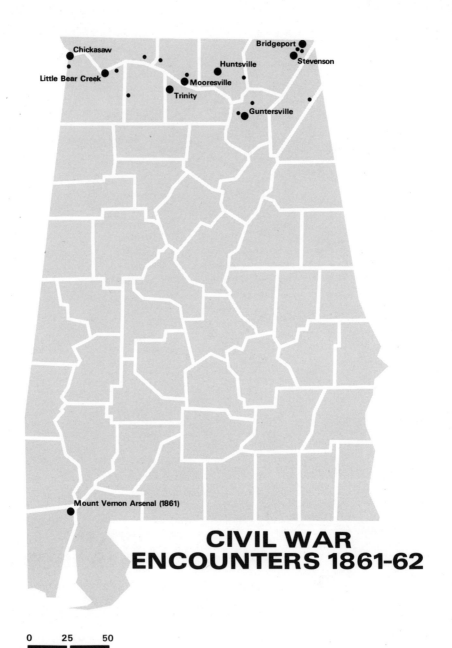

CIVIL WAR
ENCOUNTERS 1861-62

0   25   50

MILES

Florence
Tuscumbia

Day's Gap

Blount's Plantation

Black Creek
Gadsden Road

**CIVIL WAR
ENCOUNTERS 1863**

Morgan Fort

0   25   50

MILES

CIVIL WAR ENCOUNTERS 1864

Athens

Decatur

Blue Pond   Cedar Bluff

Chehaw

Gaines Fort

```
0    25    50
```
MILES

Elyton

Tuscaloosa Montevallo

Tyler Fort

Opelika

Girard

Selma

Blakely Fort

Spanish Fort

Mobile Bay

**CIVIL WAR
ENCOUNTERS 1865**

0   25   50

MILES

**TOTAL POPULATION
1860**

PERSONS

0   25   50
MILES

| 3,000-15,000 | 15,001-45,000 | 45,001-75,000 | 75,001-644,500 |

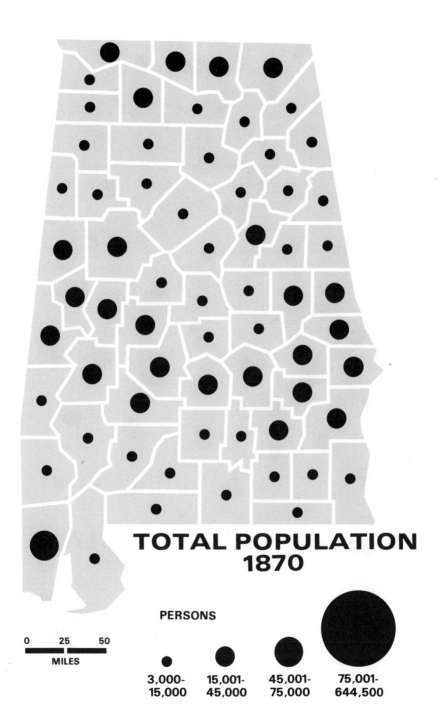

**TOTAL POPULATION
1870**

PERSONS

0   25   50
MILES

3,000-
15,000

15,001-
45,000

45,001-
75,000

75,001-
644,500

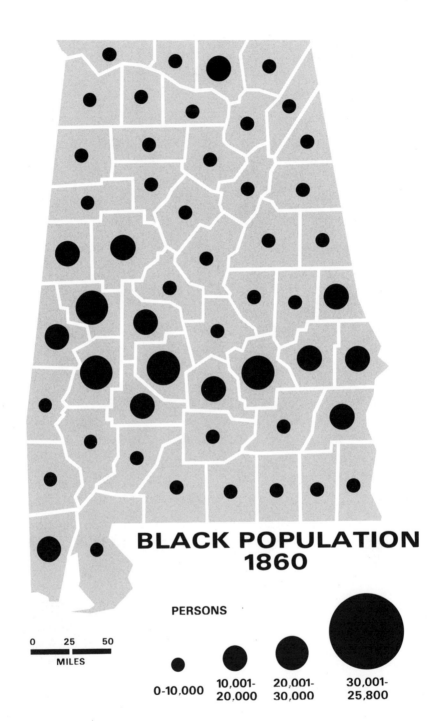

BLACK POPULATION
1860

PERSONS

0 25 50
MILES

0-10,000   10,001-   20,001-   30,001-
            20,000   30,000   25,800

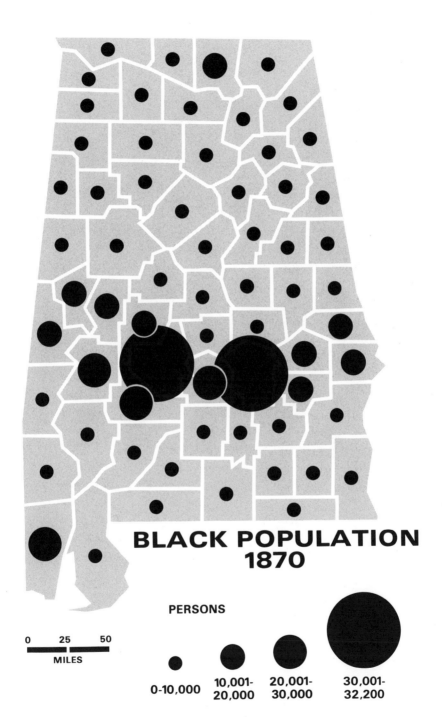

**BLACK POPULATION
1870**

PERSONS

0   25   50

MILES

0-10,000   10,001-
20,000   20,001-
30,000   30,001-
32,200

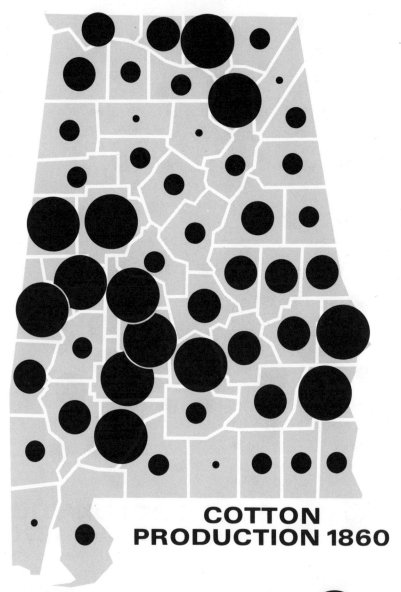

**COTTON
PRODUCTION 1860**

0   25   50
MILES

BALES (x 100)

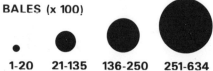

1-20   21-135   136-250   251-634

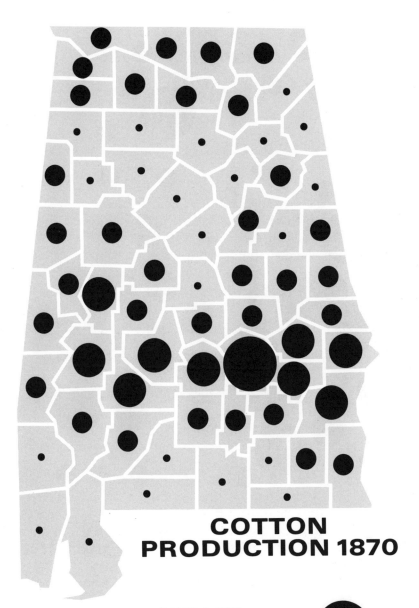

**COTTON
PRODUCTION 1870**

0   25   50

MILES

BALES (x 100)

1-20   21-135   136-250   251-634

Chapter Seven

Reconstruction, Bourbon Conservatism, and Reform 1865-1907

THROUGHOUT the political life of late 19th century Alabama, the candidate who controlled the Black Belt and the Negro votes of the State was the winning candidate. During Reconstruction the Radicals, through manipulation of the Negro majority of registered voters, maintained control. During most of the post-Reconstruction era to the turn of the century, the Democratic Party faction of "white supremacy" and Bourbon conservatism continued to control the Negro votes of the Black Belt, thus assuring defeat for the farmer movements.

In Alabama the pro-Reconstruction natives ("Scalawags") dominated Reconstruction politics with the Yankee-born politicians ("Carpetbaggers") playing a secondary role. Although the Negroes constituted a majority of registered voters during much of the era, their political leadership role was small. Alabama had no black Governors or Senators and only three black members of the U. S. House of Representatives.

In the election of 1874, the Black Belt vote supported the Radical, David P. Lewis, to remain true to form; but a North Alabama candidate, George Smith Houston, consolidated the Radical opposition, particularly the "white counties" of the state, and won by 13,190 votes. Republican rule ended in Alabama and the Democratic party was to dominate the state for the next century.

The last quarter of 19th century Alabama history is generally referred to as the Bourbon era, which featured "the rule of the brigadier generals." The pro-Confederate forces, like the House of Bourbon in France, were restored to power and a Confederate war record was practically essential for political success.

Houston, the first Democratic Governor of the era, served two consecutive two-year terms (1874-1878) as Governor and was U. S.

Senator from 1879 to 1883. He had opposed secession in 1861 and was therefore not typical of the Bourbon era. His successors were more typical.

Houston was succeeded by seven consecutive governors who had served in the Confederate Army. The senatorial seats were likewise dominated by ex-Confederates: James Pugh (1883-1897), Edmund Pettus (1897-1907), and John Tyler Morgan (1876-1907). Pettus and Morgan (both were from Selma and both died in 1907) were Confederate brigadier generals as was Governor Edward O'Neal (1882-1886).

Besides Confederate service, the Alabama Bourbons shared an appeal to white supremacy and a dedication to laissez-faire governments with low taxes and few services (including minimum aid to education). The economy-in-government position resulted in the reduction of the state debt from 30 to 10 million dollars, but the Bourbon claim to honesty in government received a severe blow in 1883, when it was learned that three-time state treasurer "Honest Ike" Vincent had fleeced the state of $230,000. After his capture in Texas (1887), he worked as a convict leasee in Birmingham coal mines before being pardoned by Governor Thomas Goode Jones in 1893.

The indifference of the Bourbons to the social ills of the day fostered opposition from the forces of reform, particularly from the economically depressed farmers of the state. The farmers were opposed to trusts, high protective tariffs, and convict leases, and favored a more equitable tax structure (a graduated income tax), more money in circulation, better schools, and direct election of U. S. Senators.

The farmer opposition to the Bourbons was expressed through various "independent movements": The Greenback Party, the Grange or Patrons of Husbandry, the Agricultural Wheel, and the Farmer's Alliance.

The Greenback Party favored the government issue of paper currency to put more money in circulation and make it easier to pay debts. They elected William M. Lowe of North Alabama to Congress in 1878, and 22 members of the State Legislature in 1882. The death of Lowe in 1882, however, deprived the party of effective leadership.

Led by state Grange leader and chairman of the State Democratic Executive Committee, W. H. Chambers, the farmers elected several pro-farm state legislators in the 1870s and 1880s, leading to a State Railroad Commission (1881), a Department of Agriculture and

Industry (1883), and some reforms in convict leases.

The Greenback Party and the Grange were followed by the Farmer's Alliance (initially called The Agricultural Wheel in Alabama), led by Reuben F. Kolb of Barbour County. Kolb was appointed State Commissioner of Agriculture in 1887. He was defeated for the Democratic nomination for Governor in 1890 and 1892 by Thomas G. Jones of Montgomery. Kolb accepted the Democratic Party decision in 1890, but in 1892 he ran as a Jeffersonian Democrat (with Populist principles). Kolb carried eight more counties than Jones but the large Black Belt vote (much of which was fraudulent, according to some Alabama historians) yielded a 11,435 majority (in a vote of almost a quarter of a million) for the Bourbon Jones.

The 1894 Kolb-Oates election was almost an "instant replay" as the one-armed Confederate hero of Henry County defeated Kolb by 27,000 votes. Again, fraud was charged but, in the absence of laws on the subject, could not be legally proven. The conservative Bourbons, manipulating the Negro voters of the Black Belt, had withstood the challenge of the reform-minded farmers for the last time. The "Brigadiers" had maintained their dominance during the last two decades of the 19th century. Progressive reform was to come with the 20th century.

**RECONSTRUCTION
VOTE 1874**

HOUSTON-LEWIS GOVERNOR'S RACE

HOUSTON PERCENT OF TOTAL VOTES

	0-24.9
	25.0-49.9
	50.0-74.9
	75.0-97.5

0   25   50

MILES

1892 POPULIST VOTE
JONES-KOLB GOVERNOR'S RACE

KOLB PERCENT OF TOTAL VOTES

0-24.9
25.0-49.9
50.0-74.9
75.0-79.1

0   25   50
MILES

● NO DATA AVAILABLE

Chapter Eight

Alabama Enters the Twentieth Century

BIRMINGHAM'S founding in 1871 and its subsequent rapid growth due to steel production had a profound effect on the total population distribution in Alabama by the turn of the century. Although in 1870 the Black Belt area had had the heaviest concentration of people with the Tennessee Valley second, by 1900 Birmingham was the most populated area of the state and Montgomery, Mobile, and Selma were vying for second place. Nevertheless, in 1900, Alabama was still predominantly rural and areas such as the Northwest Alabama hill region (especially Winston, Marion, and Fayette counties) and the forest area north and east of Mobile (Washington, Baldwin and Escambia counties) were particularly sparsely settled. These local examples of low density were not to establish the population trends of the future, however, and in the 1910-1930 era, the urbanization of Birmingham, Montgomery and Mobile was the most significant population development.

By 1900 Birmingham had also surpassed the Black Belt area in industry—a slight lead that was enlarged in the 1900-1930 years. Nineteen hundred census statistics have Mobile second, and the Montgomery-centered Black Belt industrial area sharing a third place distribution with the counties of the Tennessee Valley.

The development of improved water transportation routes also enhanced the industrial development of Alabama. The "Bourbon" Constitution of 1875 forbade state aid to this type of activity, but the National Government contributed to making Mobile Bay, the Alabama River, and the Tombigbee-Warrior system more navigable. By 1915 the cumulative developments allowed for barge traffic in iron, coal, and steel from Mobile Bay to and from Birmingham Port—a distance of about 350 miles.

Birmingham, already at the junction of two railroads, enjoyed excellent transportation with the Birmingham Port development With the favorable location of coal, iron, and limestone in close proximity, the city enlarged rapidly from its modest beginnings in 1871. Daniel Pratt was an early promotor of the "Magic City" steel complex and his son-in-law, Henry DeBardeleben, carried on the work after Pratt's death in 1873. Truman Aldrich consolidated a large part of the coal reserves in the area through his Cahaba Coal Mining Company. Enoch Ensley, James Sloss, and others promoted steel-making in the early days and, in 1907, U. S. Steel came to the "Pittsburgh of the South" with the purchase of TCI (Tennessee Coal and Iron Company). TCI, at this time, owned most of the furnaces in the city.

Birmingham's population increased in proportion to the growth of the steel industry. The city of 3,000 in 1880 increased to 26,000 in 1890 and to 38,000 in 1900—despite periodic national panics (1873, 1893, and 1907).

Other Alabama industries in the early 20th century were: textiles, cottonseed oil, commercial fertilizer, and hundreds of rural grist mills. By 1900, Alabama had more than 5,000 industrial establishments which employed more than 50,000 people.

The black population of Alabama in 1900 continued to be concentrated in the Black Belt and fringe areas but, unlike 1860, Birmingham, and Mobile, and not the Tennessee Valley, were the second ranking areas in number of black residents—a situation which extended into the World War II era. In terms of the percentage of blacks in the total population, a similar distribution held for the Black Belt area; moreover, the Tennessee Valley retained its second position in percentage of black population from 1860 to 1930.

Two conditions paralleled the heavy black population in the Black Belt—high cotton-production and a high percentage of illiteracy for the total population. In 1870 the Black Belt led the state in both categories as it did in 1900, but by 1900 there was, statewide, an increase in cotton-production and a decrease in illiteracy.

By 1900-1910 the "Wiregrass" section of southeastern Alabama began to produce more cotton, but this area declined in cotton-production in the 1910-1920 years as did the Black Belt. After 1910, the Tennessee Valley showed a marked increase in production which continued to 1930 when the Valley, in consequence of the tremendous impact of the boll weevil on South Alabama cotton production, emerged as the leading cotton-producing area of the State.

Although there was a significant decrease in the illiteracy rate statewide form 1900 to 1930, the Black Belt continued to be the area with the highest rate. The high illiteracy rate in the Black Belt for these years parallels the high percent of its total population that was black.

Under the "Bourbon" rule in the post-Reconstruction era, taxation was light and appropriations to education slim. In 1900, the average amount of education money spent on each child in Alabama was fifty cents. The national average at this time was $2.84. In 1880 25 percent of whites and 80 percent of blacks age ten years and older could not read or write. Short school terms and underpaid and underprepared teachers accounted for the slightness of the change in illiteracy by 1900. Periodic public education movements gradually lengthened the school year—to five months by 1901, to seven months by 1935, to eight months by 1943, and to the current nine months term by 1947. In the meantime Alabama ranked near the bottom of most education statistics nationally and illiteracy remained a major problem.

Higher education made some gains in the late 19th century with the establishment of Auburn University in 1872, the first normal school (teacher college) at Florence in 1872, and three black colleges—a state normal and industrial school at Huntsville (1873), Tuskegee (1881), and Alabama State (1884). Like the public schools, however, the state colleges were plagued by inadequate funding in the late 19th and early 20th centuries.

The industrial and demographic surge of Birmingham and North Alabama by the turn of the century also affected the political situation in the State. Four of the five Governors elected from 1907 to 1927 were from North Alabama and all five were more progressive in outlook than their Bourbon predecessors. All four U. S. Senators from 1907 to 1930 were also from North Alabama.

Braxton Bragg Comer of Jefferson County (Governor, 1907-1911) began the "Progressive Movement" in Alabama. His administration regulated railroads, established high schools, and passed prohibition and child labor laws. His successor, Emmet O'Neal of Florence (1911-1915), was distinguished in calling for constitutional revision, allowing cities to adopt commission governments, and providing for rural school libraries, greater safety for miners, child labor legislation, creation of the State Highway Commission, and greater aid to public schools and colleges. Charles Henderson of Pike County (1915-1919), the only South Alabamian elected Governor in the 1907-1927 years, continued the progressive trend with the organization of the Alabama Railroad Commission and a Child Welfare Department, and the passage of a Workmen's Compensation law. The administration of Anniston's Thomas E. Kilby (1919-1923) created a budget commission and passed an income tax (ruled unconstitutional by the State Supreme Court but later passed as a constitutional amendment during the Miller administration), a new Workmen's Compensation Act, and a new child labor law. Kilby also created a State Board of Education, got a $25 million bond amendment for dollar-matching with the national government on road building, and effected considerable prison reform including the construction of a modern state prison (named for him and recently destroyed), the repair of old prisons, and progress towards the abolishment of convict leasing. William "Plain Bill" Brandon of Tuscaloosa returned Alabama to the "Age of Normalcy" with his gubernatorial tenure from 1923 to 1927 but retained some of the progressive tendencies with an old age assistance law, the continuation of Kilby's road program, and the creation of the Alabama State Docks Commission.

The Senatorial seats from 1907 to 1930 were also dominated by North Alabamians with a generally progressive outlook. Edmund Pettus and John Tyler Morgan, Bourbon senators from Selma, were succeeded by North Alabamians John Hollis Bankhead, Sr., from Jasper and Joseph F. Johnston of Birmingham (a lawyer in Selma for 17 years). Bankhead was instrumental in securing federal money to dredge Mobile Harbor and improve navigation on the Tombigbee River (paving the way for the Mobile to Birmingham Port navigation) and for the framing and passage of the Federal Good Roads Act of 1916 by which federal money was provided on a 50-50 matching basis with the states. Bankhead also had two sons who played a major role in New Deal legislation. After Johnston died in 1913, Oscar Underwood of Birmingham (Democratic floor leader in the U. S. House for Wilson and a major force in the passage of the Federal Reserve Act and the Underwood-Simmons Tariff) was elected Senator. Underwood's senatorial career was highlighted by his opposition to prohibition and the Ku Klux Klan, both positions partially responsible for the failure of his plans to secure the Democratic Presidential nomination in 1924. Bankhead died in 1920 and was succeeded by "Cotton Tom" Heflin of Lafayette, who served until defeated by John Hollis Bankhead, Jr., in 1930.

Thus North Alabama and progressivism dominated the Alabama economic, demographic, and political life in the first three decades of the 20th century. The State became accustomed to providing greater services for its people, and a beginning was made in improving the socio-economic status of the residents—an effort which was continued in the post-1927 period by the progressive administrations of South Alabamians Bibb Graves, Gordon Persons, and George Wallace.

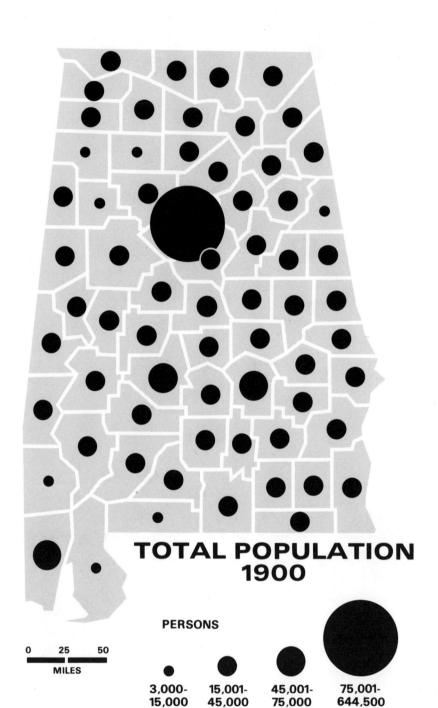

TOTAL POPULATION 1900

PERSONS

0   25   50
MILES

| 3,000-15,000 | 15,001-45,000 | 45,001-75,000 | 75,001-644,500 |

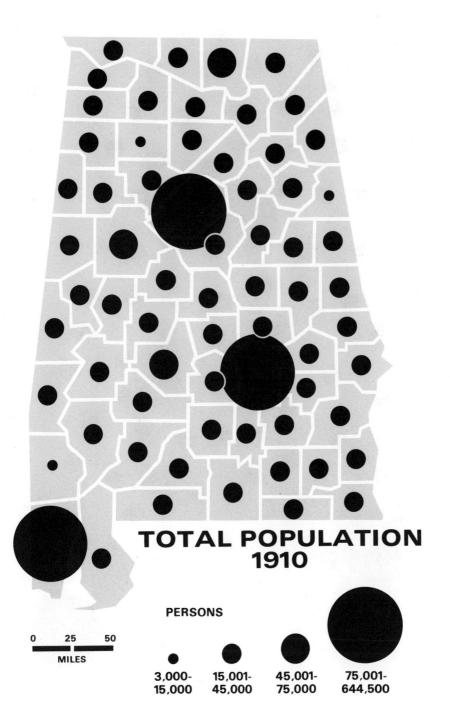

**TOTAL POPULATION
1910**

PERSONS

0   25   50
MILES

3,000-
15,000

15,001-
45,000

45,001-
75,000

75,001-
644,500

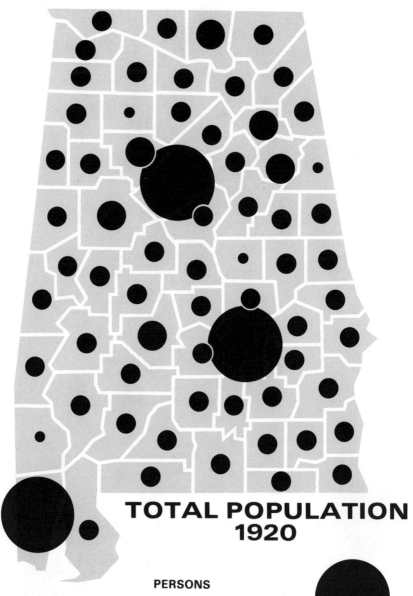

**TOTAL POPULATION
1920**

PERSONS

0   25   50

MILES

| 3,000-
15,000 | 15,001-
45,000 | 45,001-
75,000 | 75,001-
644,500 |

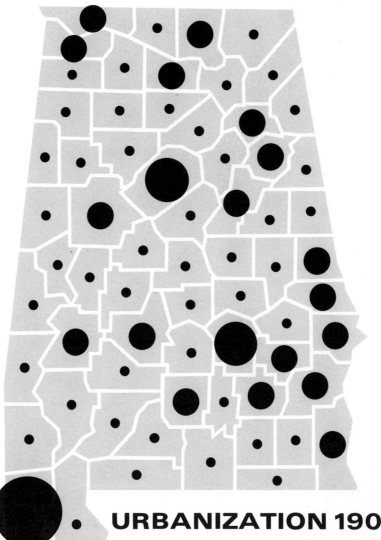

URBANIZATION 1900

PERCENT OF TOTAL POPULATION
LIVING IN TOWNS OF 2,500 OR MORE

0   25   50

MILES

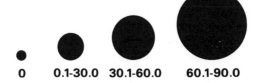

0   0.1-30.0   30.1-60.0   60.1-90.0

INDUSTRY 1900
VALUE ADDED BY MANUFACTURING

DOLLARS

0   25   50
MILES

0-50,000   50,001-
100,000   100,001-
300,000   300,001-
835,000

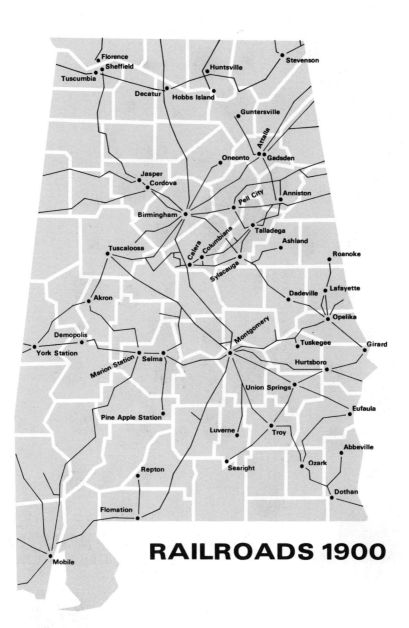

RAILROADS 1900

MILES

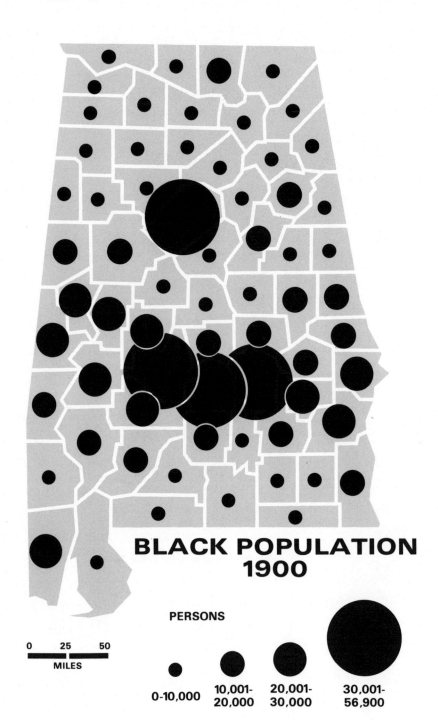

**BLACK POPULATION
1900**

PERSONS

0   25   50

MILES

0-10,000   10,001-
20,000   20,001-
30,000   30,001-
56,900

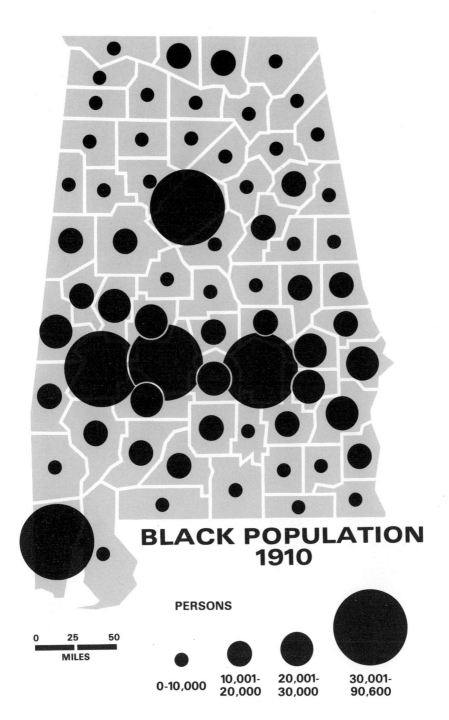

**BLACK POPULATION
1910**

PERSONS

0 25 50
MILES

0-10,000 10,001-
20,000 20,001-
30,000 30,001-
90,600

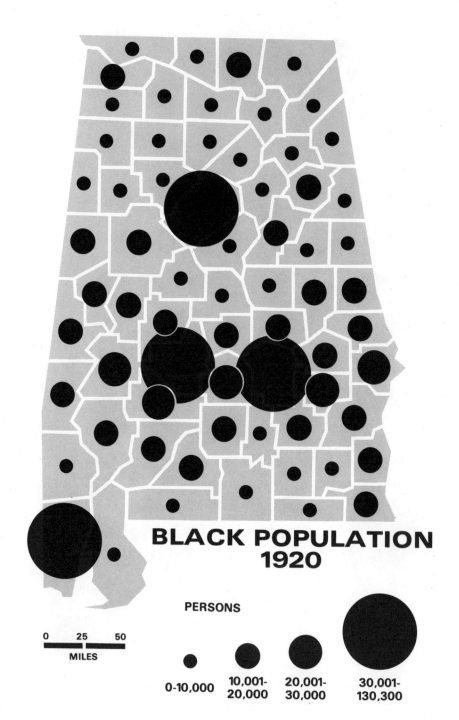

**BLACK POPULATION
1920**

PERSONS

0   25   50
MILES

0-10,000

10,001-
20,000

20,001-
30,000

30,001-
130,300

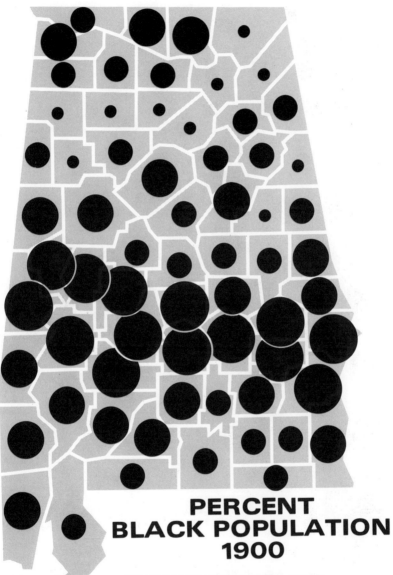

PERCENT BLACK POPULATION 1900

PERCENT OF TOTAL POPULATION

0   25   50

MILES

0-12.0   12.1-36.0   36.1-60.0   60.1-90.0

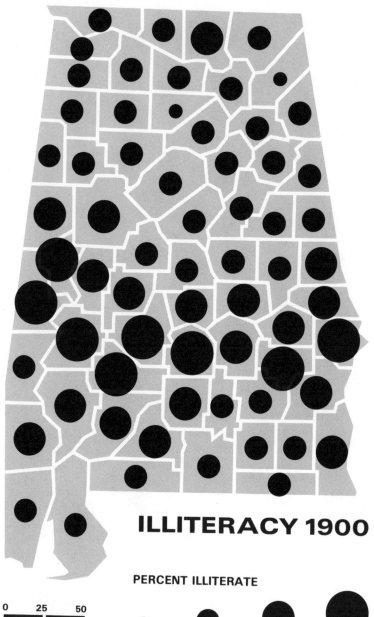

ILLITERACY 1900

PERCENT ILLITERATE

0   25   50
MILES

5.1-12.0   12.1-24.0   24.1-36.0   36.1-52.0

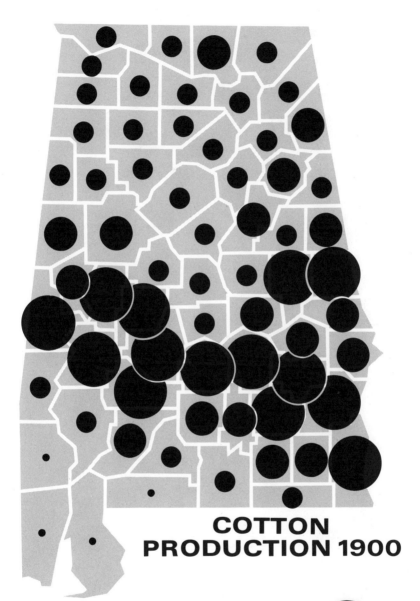

**COTTON
PRODUCTION 1900**

0   25   50
MILES

BALES (x 100)

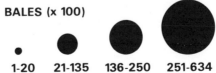

1-20   21-135   136-250   251-634

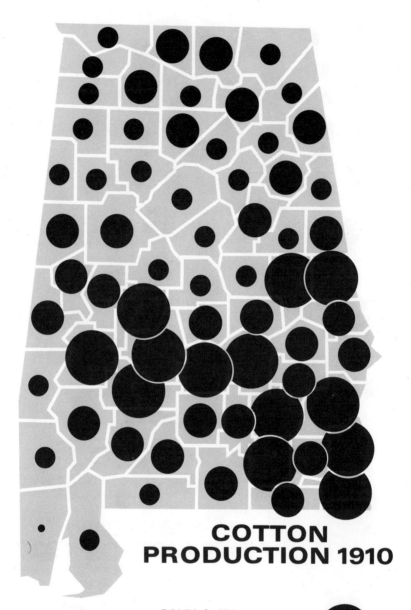

**COTTON
PRODUCTION 1910**

BALES (x 100)

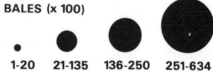

1-20   21-135   136-250   251-634

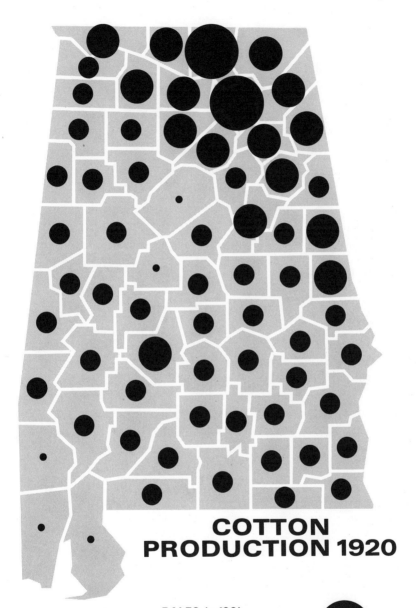

**COTTON
PRODUCTION 1920**

0   25   50

MILES

BALES (x 100)

1-20   21-135   136-250   251-634

Chapter Nine

Alabama in Depression and War 1930-1950

THE North Alabama and progressive domination of the U. S. Senatorial positions during the first three decades of the 20th century was maintained throughout the Depression, New Deal, World War II, and post-WW II eras. Lister Hill of Montgomery was the only South Alabama Senator from 1907 to the present and he was one of the more progressive 20th century Senators.

Hugo Black of Birmingham followed Underwood as U. S. Senator and served until President Roosevelt appointed him to the Supreme Court in 1937. Governor Bibb Graves appointed his wife Dixie to take Black's seat in the Senate but shortly before the 1938 election he appointed Lister Hill of Montgomery to the seat. Hill was a very progressive Senator who, in his thirty years in the Senate (1938-1968), was known for legislation supporting labor, TVA, and federal aid to education, health, and hospitals, including the Hill-Burton Act, which made federal funds available for the building of hospitals. Hill voluntarily retired from politics in 1968 and was succeeded by Jim Allen of Gadsden.

The other Senate seat was occupied by Tom Heflin from 1920 to 1930—from the death of John Hollis Bankhead, Sr., to his defeat by John Hollis Bankhead, Jr. Bankhead served until 1946 when he was succeeded by John Sparkman of Huntsville. J. H. Bankhead, Jr., and his younger brother, Will B. Bankhead (U. S. House of Representatives, 1916-1940) were prominent members of the New Deal administration of President Roosevelt. John Hollis coauthored the Bankhead-Jones Farm Tenant Act of 1937, authored the Bankhead Cotton Act, and played a major role in developing the Agricultural Adjustment Acts. William was Speaker of the House from 1936 to his death in 1940.

Whereas North Alabamians dominated the Senatorial seats in the three decades before and after 1930, the opposite was true for the Governorship of the State. From the beginning of the Bibb Graves' first administration in 1927 through the current administration of George Wallace, there have been only three North Alabamians in the Governor's chair: Frank Dixon of Jefferson County (1939-1943); Jim Folsom of Cullman County (1947-1951; 1955-1959) and "Big Jim" was born in Coffee County (the "Wiregrass" section of South Alabama); and Albert Brewer of Decatur (1968-1970) who, as Lieutenant Governor, succeeded to the governorship on the death of Lurleen Wallace.

The South Alabama gubernatorial supremacy did not mean consistent Bourbon or conservative administrations, however, as the tenures of Bibb Graves, Gordon Persons (1951-1955), and George Wallace illustrate. During his two terms, Graves instituted a state-supported minimum public education program for every county in the state that greatly boosted the quality of education in the poorer counties. The Graves' administration also made the largest education appropriation in the State's history (later surpassed by the Folsom, Persons, and the Wallace administrations). Graves was able to get bills for a minimum school year of seven months (extended to nine months under Folsom), and free textbooks through the fourth grade (extended through the twelfth grade under Wallace). Graves' success was due in part to the circumstance of his being Governor before the Depression and, in his second term, after the New Deal programs were beginning to have some effect.

The Governors during the hard years of the Depression and World War II had less success, as might have been expected. As Governor during the initial years of the Great Depression, Benjamin Meek Miller (1931-1934) was not able to continue the Graves spending (if he had had the inclination to do so) but he was known for wise economic moves such as a state income tax via constitutional amendment, a Budget Control Act to keep the State from spending more than it receives, and a consulting study by the Brookings Institution which resulted in the State merit system and other reforms in State administration.

Alabama's World War II Governors were Frank Dixon (1939-1943) and Chauncey Sparks (1943-1947). Dixon added to Miller's efforts to streamline Alabama government—primarily by the creation of departments which were responsible to the Governor. Sparks, a darkhorse candidate elected after the favorite, Bibb Graves, died during the campaign, was mainly known for his fight against freight rate discrimination.

From a demographic and economic standpoint, North Alabama had clearly replaced South Alabama as the State's leader by 1930. Birmingham was the leading area of the State in population, personal wealth (per capita income), and industrial production; and the Tennessee Valley had emerged as the leading cotton-producing area of Alabama. The Black Belt still led in the number of blacks, the highest percent of blacks in the total population, and the highest percent of illiteracy—Black Belt statistics that prevail currently. Of course, the Southeastern United States, and Alabama as a part of it, was still, in the 1938 words of President Franklin D. Roosevelt, "the number one economic problem" of the country.

Although the Birmingham, Montgomery, and Mobile areas continued to be the major population centers in 1930, secondary population centers began to emerge, such as Dothan, Tuscaloosa, Jasper, and the Huntsville-Decatur, Gadsden-Anniston, and Selma areas. Additionally, by 1940, the Birmingham to Tuscaloosa area showed a marked increase in population.

Birmingham was clearly the top industrial area of the State by 1930 but some industrial development had also taken place in the Huntsville-Decatur and Gadsden-Anniston-Talladega areas, in the Piedmont (Randolph and Clay counties), and in Montgomery, Selma, Mobile, Escambia County, and Choctaw County. The industrial centers were also served well by railroads.

The Tennessee Valley led in cotton production for the first time in the State's history, but the Black Belt and the "Wiregrass" had increased their production some since 1920. The Tennessee Valley remained the center of production from 1930 through 1970 although there were fluctuations statewide such as the general decline in 1940 and the general increase in 1950.

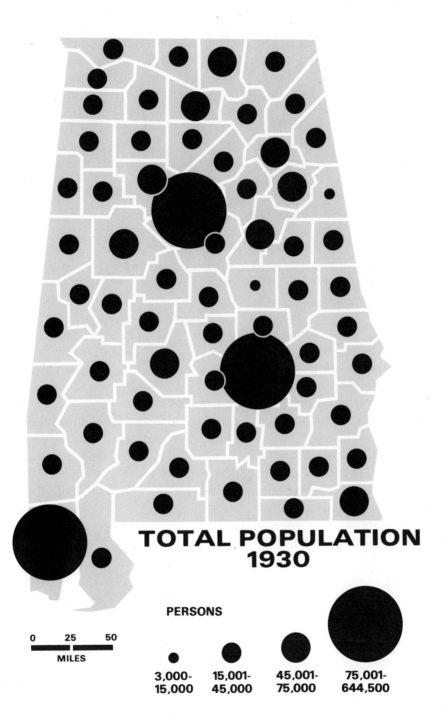

**TOTAL POPULATION
1930**

PERSONS

0   25   50
MILES

3,000-
15,000

15,001-
45,000

45,001-
75,000

75,001-
644,500

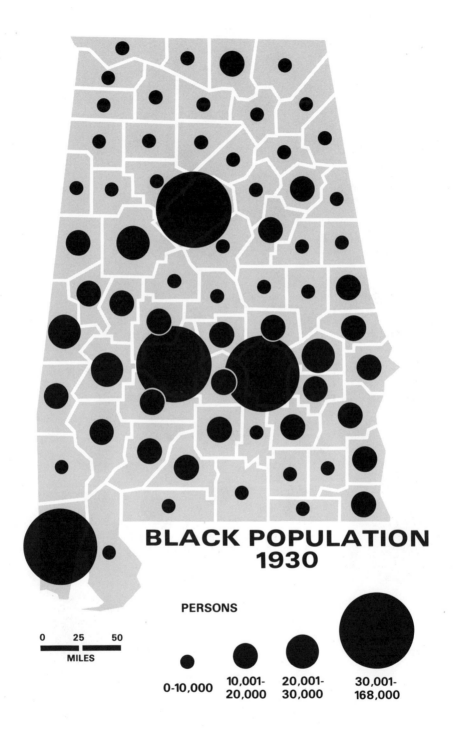

**BLACK POPULATION
1930**

PERSONS

0   25   50
MILES

0-10,000   10,001-
20,000   20,001-
30,000   30,001-
168,000

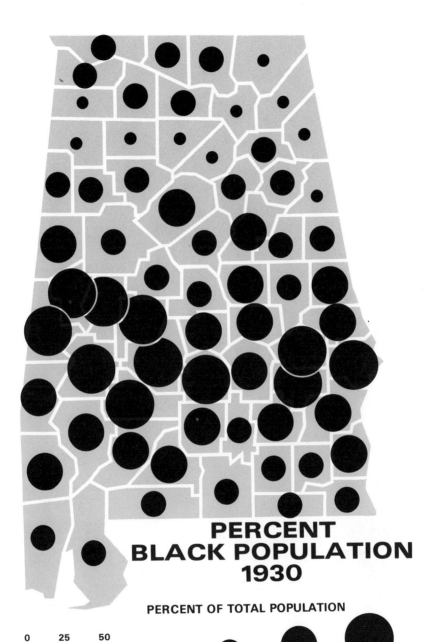

**PERCENT
BLACK POPULATION
1930**

PERCENT OF TOTAL POPULATION

0   25   50

MILES

0-12.0   12.1-36.0   36.1-60.0   60.1-90.0

URBANIZATION 1930

PERCENT OF TOTAL POPULATION
LIVING IN TOWNS OF 2,500 OR MORE

0   25   50
MILES

0   0.1-30.0   30.1-60.0   60.1-90.0

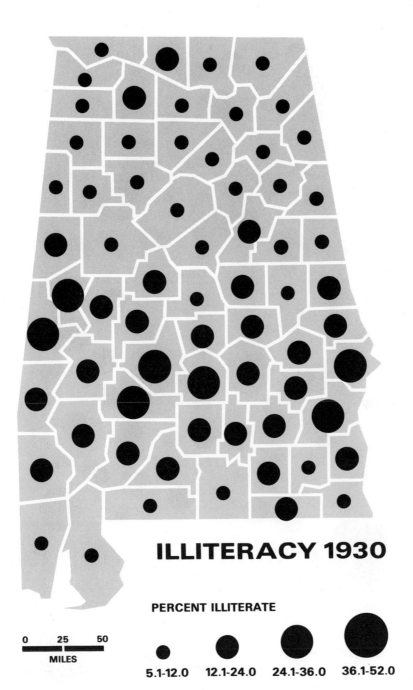

ILLITERACY 1930

PERCENT ILLITERATE

0   25   50
MILES

5.1-12.0   12.1-24.0   24.1-36.0   36.1-52.0

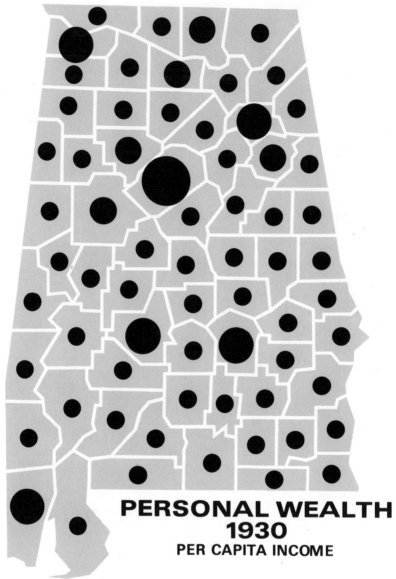

**PERSONAL WEALTH
1930**
PER CAPITA INCOME

DOLLARS

0   25   50

MILES

156-
285

286-
410

411-
540

541-
664

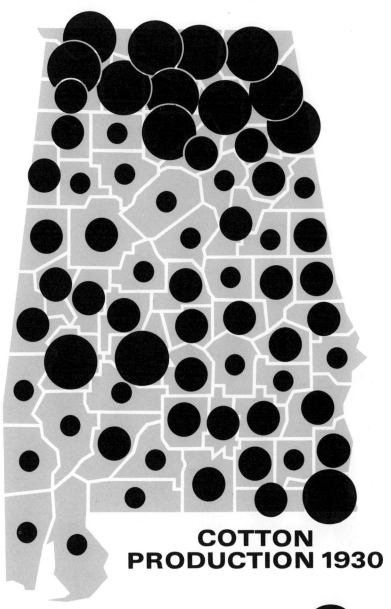

**COTTON
PRODUCTION 1930**

0   25   50
MILES

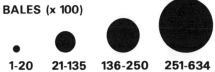

BALES (x 100)

1-20   21-135   136-250   251-634

INDUSTRY 1930
VALUE ADDED BY MANUFACTURING

DOLLARS

0   25   50
MILES

0-50,000   50,001-   100,001-   300,001-
            100,000   300,000   835,000

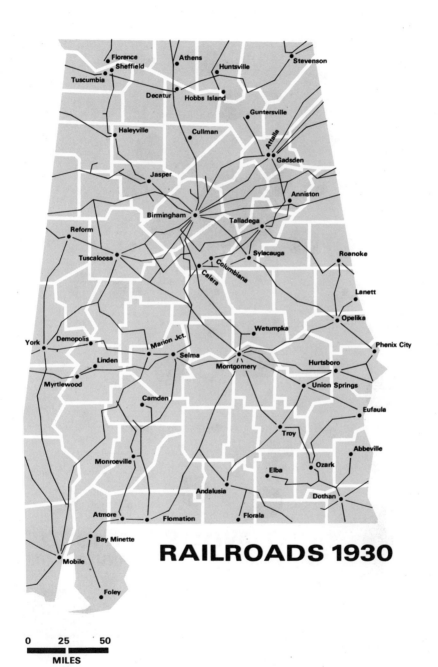

RAILROADS 1930

0   25   50
MILES

**TOTAL POPULATION
1930**

PERSONS

0   25   50
MILES

3,000-
15,000

15,001-
45,000

45,001-
75,000

75,001-
644,500

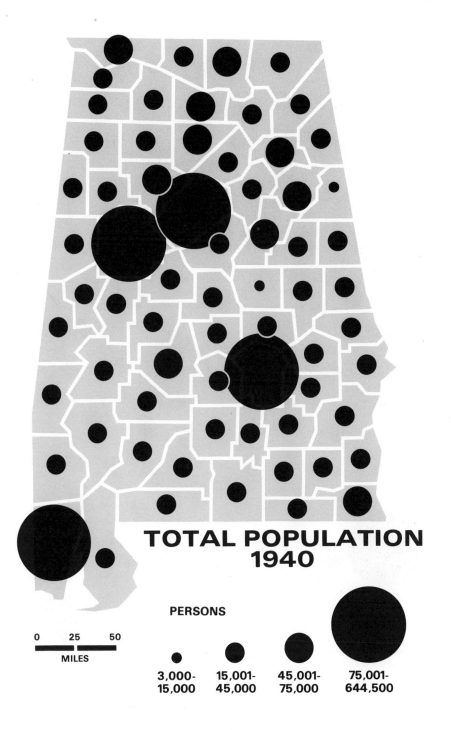

**TOTAL POPULATION
1940**

PERSONS

0   25   50
MILES

3,000-
15,000

15,001-
45,000

45,001-
75,000

75,001-
644,500

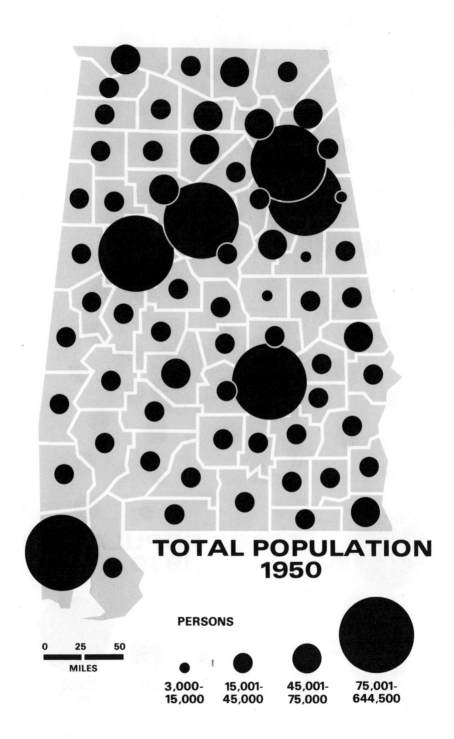

**TOTAL POPULATION
1950**

PERSONS

0   25   50
MILES

| 3,000-15,000 | 15,001-45,000 | 45,001-75,000 | 75,001-644,500 |

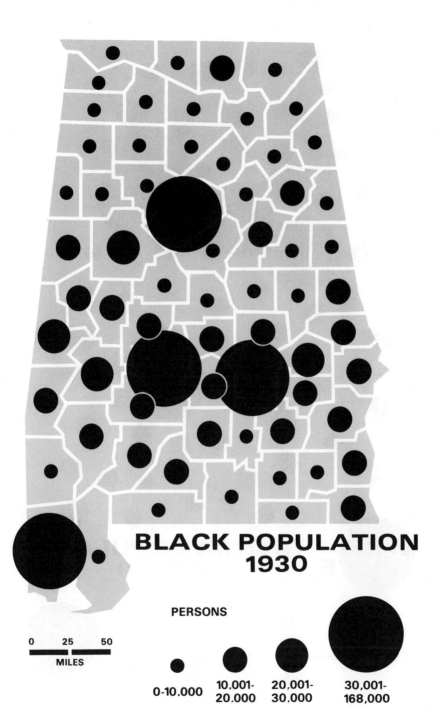

**BLACK POPULATION
1930**

PERSONS

0-10,000   10,001-
20,000   20,001-
30,000   30,001-
168,000

0   25   50
MILES

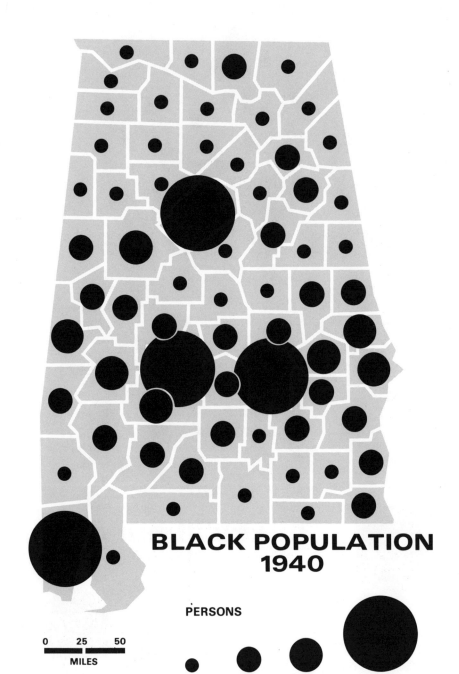

**BLACK POPULATION
1940**

PERSONS

0   25   50
MILES

0-10,000   10,001-
20,000   20,001-
30,000   30,001-
179,200

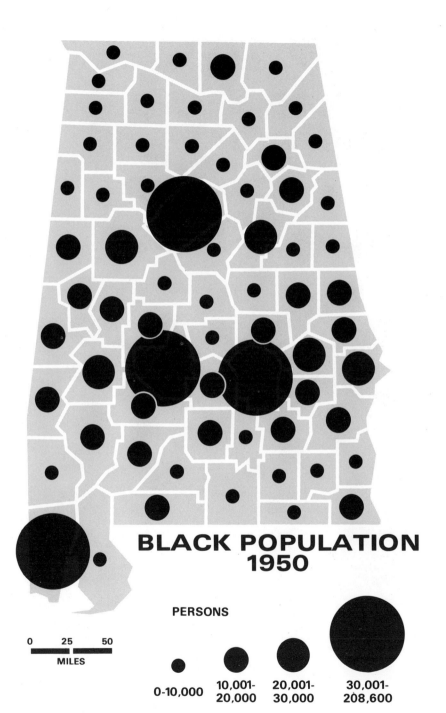

**BLACK POPULATION
1950**

PERSONS

0   25   50

MILES

0-10,000

10,001-
20,000

20,001-
30,000

30,001-
208,600

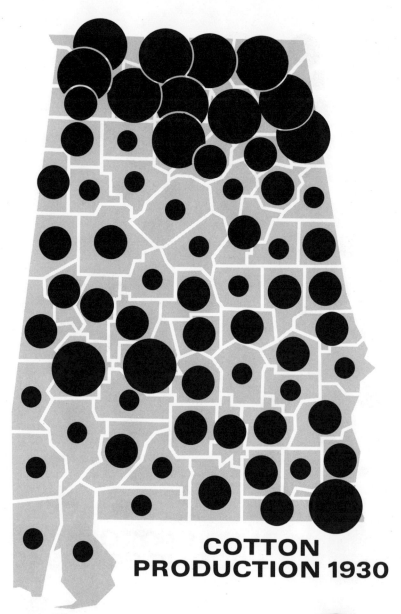

**COTTON
PRODUCTION 1930**

0   25   50
MILES

BALES (x 100)

1-20   21-135   136-250   251-634

[107]

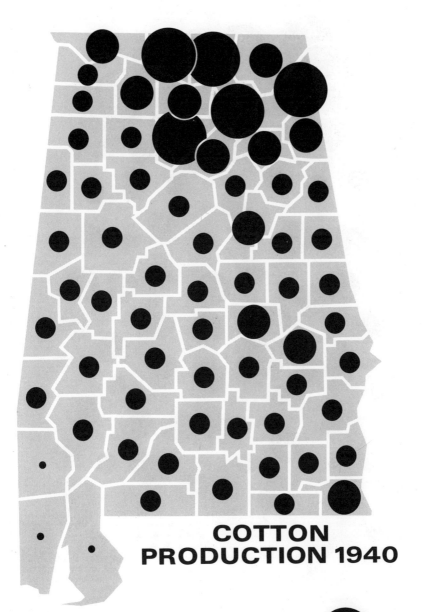

**COTTON
PRODUCTION 1940**

0 25 50
MILES

BALES (x 100)

1-20   21-135   136-250   251-634

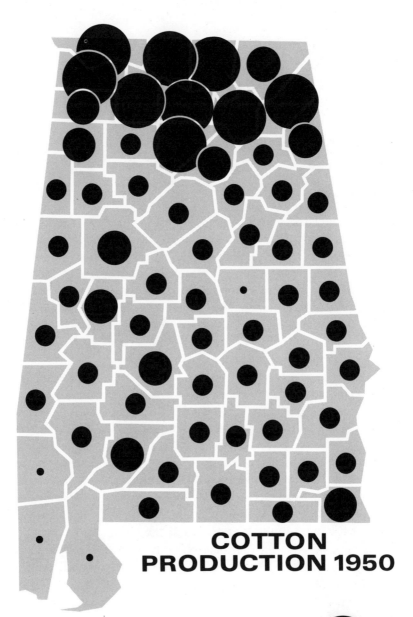

COTTON PRODUCTION 1950

0   25   50
MILES

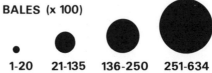

BALES (x 100)

1-20   21-135   136-250   251-634

Chapter Ten

Alabama Politics After World War II

IN 1946, "Big Jim" Folsom (6'8'' and 245 pounds), accompanied by a hillbilly band, made more than 300 "turnip greens and corn bread" type speeches throughout Alabama. His homespun campaign speeches included promises for teacher raises, old-age pensions, constitutional revision to reapportion the legislature and repeal the poll tax, rural roads, and getting tough with the "Big Mules" (the interests). Although he faced a hostile legislature after his election, Folsom was able to get bills for a teacher raise, a nine-months school term, a small old-age pension, and an antimasking law against the KKK. His administration was also known for the building of 3,000 miles of farm-to-market roads. Folsom's second administration was marked by another teacher's raise, a $110 million bond amendment for school buildings, a Competitive Bid Act, $250 million expenditures on farm-to-market roads, a general anti-segregation stand, increased rate of industrialization, expansion of the State Docks, and a considerable welfare program which included legislation to get federal funds for hospitals under the Hill-Burton Act, the establishment of the Pensions and Security Department, and additional services for the mentally ill, the deaf, and the blind.

The Governor who served between the two Folsom terms was Gordon Persons (1951-1955). Persons had good relations with the legislature and secured bills to raise teachers' salaries, to establish the first statewide educational television network in the nation, to appropriate $1 million for health and welfare, and to float bond issues of $25 million for roads and of $100 million for school construction.

Toward the close of Folsom's second administration, the gubernatorial election of 1958 took place. As no candidate received a majority in the primary, a "runoff" was staged between Attorney

General John Patterson and Circuit Court Judge George Wallace. Patterson's father, Albert J., had been murdered in 1954 after being nominated for Attorney General on a "clean-up Phenix City" platform. John was subsequently selected for the nomination and, as Attorney General, pursued the "clean-up of Phenix City" with Governor Persons and a special circuit judge, Walter B. Jones of Montgomery. As Attorney General, Patterson also acquired a segregation image for his opposition to the NAACP, his defense of segregated public schools, and the black boycotts of buses in Montgomery and stores in Tuskegee. Wallace, a former legislator and Folsom supporter before becoming Circuit Judge, shared a segregationist position with Patterson, but his position was not so widely publicized. Patterson won by 315,353 votes to 250,451 votes for Wallace.

Patterson's administration secured a $100 million bond issue for classroom construction, a $60 million bond amendment for roads, a $7 million bond issue for inland dock construction in the Tennessee Valley, and a 10 percent tax on whiskey to be divided between mental health and old age assistance.

Wallace won the 1962 election in a runoff with Ryan DeGraffenried of Tuscaloosa and has dominated Alabama politics since that date. The Wallace administrations have supported education, highways, and aid to the handicapped, and have attracted industry to the State. In his first term, Wallace obtained an additional annual appropriation of $44 million for education. In 1965 he added a $116 million bond issue for education and subsequently he has launched a statewide program of post-high school educational facilities which have yielded twelve junior colleges and eighteen vocational schools and, as noted earlier, free textbooks through the twelfth grade. He also secured a $110 million bond issue for highway construction.

When a 1966 constitutional amendment, which would have allowed him to succeed himself in office, was defeated in the Senate, Wallace ran his wife Lurleen, who won the 1966 gubernatorial without need for a runoff. Mrs. Wallace's administration was, of course, a continuation of the Wallace program of the first administration but, on her own initiative, the mental health program of the State was strengthened. Albert Brewer, as mentioned earlier, became Governor on Lurleen's death in 1968, but he was defeated by Wallace two years later in a very close runoff.

In addition to serving as Governor of the State, Wallace has been actively engaged in national politics. Alabamians had shown a tendency to buck the "Solid South" tag of constant support for the Democratic Party on a number of occasions: in 1928, Hoover lacked only 7,072 votes of carrying the State (attributable to a protest vote against Democrat Al Smith—a Catholic, a wet, and a product of the sidewalks of New York); in 1948, the state was carried by the Dixiecrat slate of Senator Strom Thurmond of South Carolina and Governor Fielding Wright of Mississippi (a reaction to the strong civil rights plank in the Democratic candidate's platform); and in 1964, the state supported Republican conservative Barry Goldwater and elected five Republicans in their U. S. House delegation of seven.

Republicans capitalized on some of the anti-Democratic Party sentiment by electing mayors in Mobile and Birmingham and Congressmen in the Mobile, Montgomery, and Birmingham districts. The "urban Republicanism" first appearing during the Eisenhower years, was weakened by post-1948 Democratic Party actions such as the Vice-Presidential nomination going to Alabama U. S. Senator John Sparkman in 1952. (Sparkman had sponsored national legislation in favor of labor, TVA, and middle income housing.)

The major "Dixiecrat-type" revolt of the 1960s, however, was captured by Governor Wallace. Wallace entered Presidential primaries in 1964 and secured more than 30 percent of the vote in Wisconsin and Indiana and 42 percent of the vote in Maryland. Known for his 1963 "stand in the schoolhouse door" at the University of Alabama, Wallace hoped, by a favorable showing in the primaries, to defeat the Civil Rights Act of 1964. The Act passed and, following the Selma March of 1965, a Civil Rights Act of 1965 was also passed. In 1968, Wallace entered the Presidential race as a third-party candidate and, to the amazement of many national political observors, carried five states (Arkansas, Louisiana, Mississippi, Alabama, and Georgia). A third national effort, in the Presidential race of 1972, was cut short by the near-assassination of Governor Wallace following a speech in Maryland.

Wallace's showing in the 1968 and 1972 Presidential races, while not accomplishing possible goals of throwing the election into the House of Representatives, did contribute to the voicing of subsequent positions by President Nixon that were very similar to those of Alabama's Governor. Furthermore, the overwhelming defeat of the Democratic nominee in 1972, George McGovern, who captured the nomination despite opposition from Wallace and other national conservatives, suggests that the Democratic Party will lean more in the Wallace direction in the 1976 election. Any way one looks at it, he would have to admit that Alabama's "fighting judge" had made a tremendous impact on Alabama and national politics in the last decade.

This impact is more notable from the fact that, in the same years, Alabama's Congressional clout has lessened. John Sparkman retains a senior position in the Senate due to his tenure since 1946, but the overall Congressional strength is less due to the 1968 retirement of Lister Hill and the loss of two Congressmen via reapportionment (the two who lost in statewide balloting were Frank Boykin of Mobile, who had been in Congress since 1935 and Carl Elliott of Jasper, a veteran of eighteen years House service). The current delegation is composed of Senators Sparkman and Allen and House members Jack Edwards (Rep., Mobile), Bill Dickinson (Rep., Montgomery), Bill Nichols (Dem., Sylacauga), John Buchanan (Rep., Birmingham), Walter Flowers (Dem., Sylacauga), Tom Bevill (Dem., Jasper), and Bob Jones (Dem., Scottsboro).

**WALLACE
PATTERSON
RUN-OFF 1958**

WALLACE PERCENT OF TOTAL VOTES

20.0-34.9

35.0-49.9

50.0-64.9

65.0-95.0

0   25   50

MILES

**WALLACE
DE GRAFFENRIED
RUN-OFF 1962**

WALLACE PERCENT OF TOTAL VOTES

20.0-34.9
35.0-49.9
50.0-64.9
65.0-95.0

0   25   50
MILES

MRS. WALLACE PRIMARY VOTE 1966

MRS. WALLACE PERCENT OF TOTAL VOTES

20.0-34.9
35.0-49.9
50.0-64.9
65.0-95.0

0   25   50
MILES

**WALLACE-BREWER
RUN-OFF 1970**

WALLACE PERCENT OF TOTAL VOTES

20.0-34.9

35.0-49.9

50.0-64.9

65.0-95.0

0   25   50

MILES

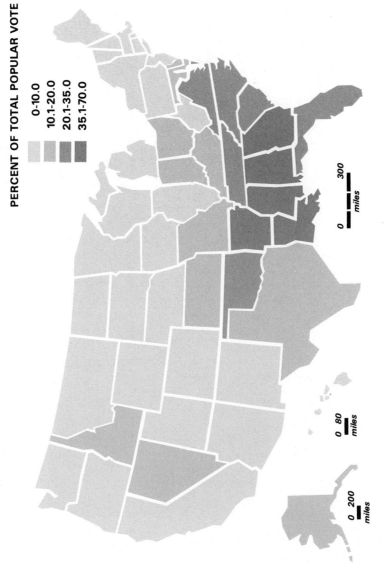

WALLACE VOTE FOR PRESIDENT 1968

PERCENT OF TOTAL POPULAR VOTE

0-10.0
10.1-20.0
20.1-35.0
35.1-70.0

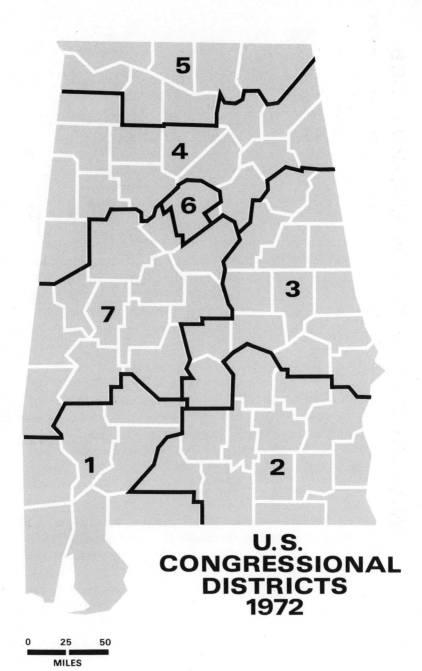

**U.S.
CONGRESSIONAL
DISTRICTS
1972**

0 25 50
MILES

Chapter Eleven

Alabama Industry and Population After World War II

THE trends of the 1930-1950 era of depression and world war continued into the era after World War II. By the 1960s the State as a whole was more urban than rural (more people living in urban areas than in rural areas) and Birmingham, Montgomery, and Mobile were clearly urban. The Gadsden-Anniston area showed a surge in population in 1950 and this tendency has continued through 1970. The greatest increase in the two decades since 1950, however, was in the Huntsville-Decatur area. Huntsville replaced Montgomery as the third largest city in the State in 1970. Almost one-half of the State's people now live in the six largest metropolitan areas of Birmingham, Mobile, Huntsville, Montgomery, Tuscaloosa, and Gadsden.

The black population also showed the impact of urbanization and the greatest concentrations of blacks in the State were in the urban areas of Birmingham, Mobile, and Montgomery. The Black Belt still led in the percent of blacks in the total population—a particularly relevant political statistic after the massive black voter registration following the Civil Rights Act of 1965. There continues to be an emigration of blacks from Alabama, however, as evidenced by the decline in the percentage of blacks in the total State population—from almost 50 percent in 1880 to less than 36 percent in 1930 to 30 percent in 1960.

Birmingham continued to be the industrial leader in the State, but the Huntsville-Decatur area showed an industrial boom since the 1950s and the Gadsden-Anniston area shared third place with Mobile. Birmingham's major industry is still iron and steel, and U. S. Steel retains its dominance in the local industry. Gadsden also has a significant steel production—with Republic Steel the major company—but tire and tube plants are likewise important local industries. Anniston is mainly known for its cast iron pipe; and Huntsville, "The

Rocket City," for the space age technology centered at Redstone Arsenal and NASA (National Aeronautics and Space Administration). Textiles remain significant in Alabama industry—particularly in northeast and east-central Alabama (including the industries in the valley of the Chattahoochee).

Alabama currently ranks twentieth in the United States in the production of minerals—and third in the states of the Confederate South. Leading distributions include: coal in Jefferson, Walker, and Tuscaloosa counties; stone statewide, but Sylacauga marble is particularly well known; cement statewide; and oil in southwest Alabama—with 71 percent of the State's production coming from the Citronelle Field in Mobile County.

Alabama industry is stimulated by power resources and transportation developments. TVA and Alabama Power Company facilities contribute to Alabama's being ranked fifth in the United States in developed electric power. Transportation advantages include: more than 1,000 miles of navigable waterways (fourth nationally), 7,000 miles of paved roads, almost 5,000 miles of railroads, and airlines serving the major urban areas.

The urban areas also led in formal education and personal wealth. The Black Belt—particularly the western and southern parts—was lowest in education and personal wealth.

The Tennessee Valley still led in cotton production, but the Black Belt increased its production, and its relative standing statewide, since 1950. By 1960 Tennessee Valley production ranked third in the South behind the Mississippi Delta and the prairielands of East Texas. The statewide cotton increase in the past three decades is due to greater yields—less than one-half bale per acre in 1930 to more than a bale per acre in 1965.

But the State as a whole is much more diversified agriculturally than in earlier years. Cotton sales now constitute only about 23 percent of total farm sales. The "Wiregrass" of Southeast Alabama shifted to peanuts (often paralleled by hog production) after the boll weevil hit cotton in the 1910s, and the town of Enterprise erected a monument to the insect responsible for this agricultural diversification. The Black Belt has become the major beef and dairy cattle area of Alabama (Tennessee Valley second), and the hill country of North Alabama is the State's poultry center. Corn and soybeans, a recently popular crop of Alabama farmers, are grown all over the State.

Despite these transitions from the rural, agricultural economy to an urban, industrial economy and the accompanying gains in standard of living and education, Alabama remains far behind the nation in several areas. In the 1960s the State ranked 46th in housing, 47th in per capita income, and 45th in education. A look at the past is sometimes discouraging, but as Herbert Hoover said in his 1928 inaugural address, "The future is bright with hope."

**TOTAL POPULATION
1970**

PERSONS

0   25   50
MILES

| 3,000-
15,000 | 15,001-
45,000 | 45,001-
75,000 | 75,001-
644,500 |

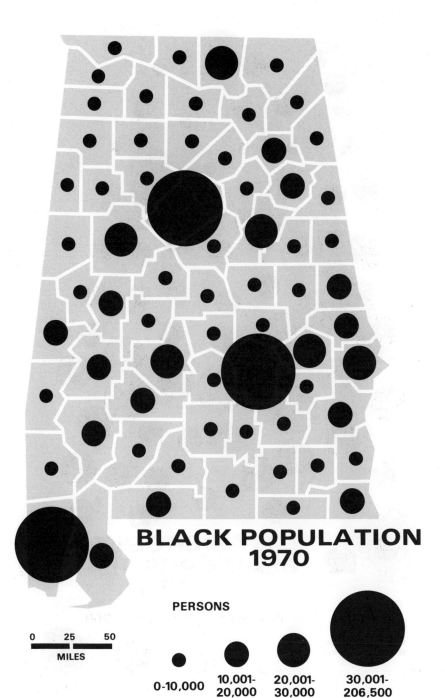

**BLACK POPULATION
1970**

PERSONS

0 25 50
MILES

0-10,000   10,001-
20,000

20,001-
30,000

30,001-
206,500

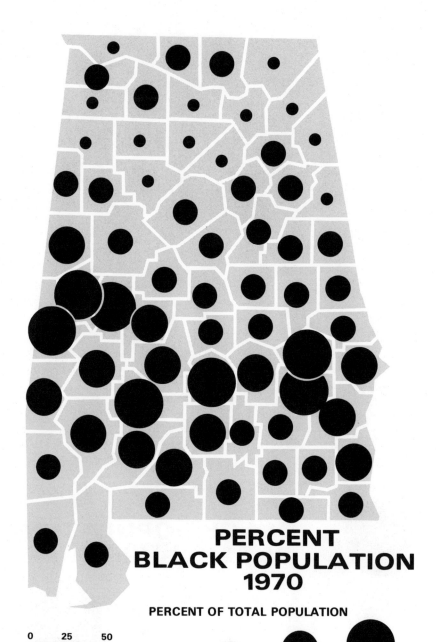

PERCENT BLACK POPULATION 1970

PERCENT OF TOTAL POPULATION

0   25   50

MILES

0-12.0   12.1-36.0   36.1-60.0   60.1-90.0

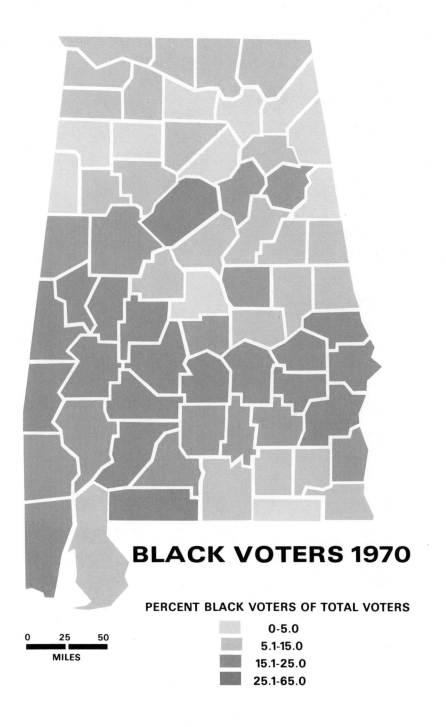

BLACK VOTERS 1970

PERCENT BLACK VOTERS OF TOTAL VOTERS

0-5.0

5.1-15.0

15.1-25.0

25.1-65.0

0   25   50

MILES

**POPULATION
CHANGE 1950–1970**

DECREASED FROM

3801-7600

0-3800

INCREASED FROM

0-20,000

20,001-113,600

0   25   50

MILES

URBANIZATION 1970

PERCENT OF TOTAL POPULATION
LIVING IN TOWNS OF 2,500 OR MORE

0   25   50
MILES

0   0.1-30.0   30.1-60.0   60.1-90.0

INDUSTRY 1970
VALUE ADDED BY MANUFACTURING

DOLLARS

0   25   50
MILES

0-50,000

50,001-
100,000

100,001-
300,000

300,001-
835,000

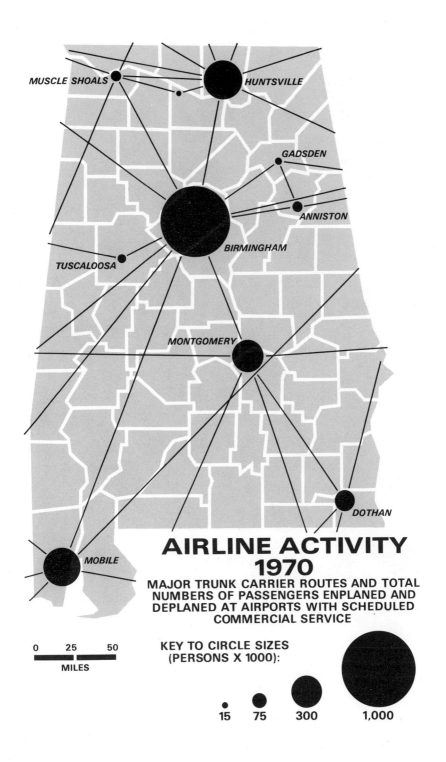

MUSCLE SHOALS

HUNTSVILLE

GADSDEN

ANNISTON

BIRMINGHAM

TUSCALOOSA

MONTGOMERY

DOTHAN

MOBILE

AIRLINE ACTIVITY
1970
MAJOR TRUNK CARRIER ROUTES AND TOTAL
NUMBERS OF PASSENGERS ENPLANED AND
DEPLANED AT AIRPORTS WITH SCHEDULED
COMMERCIAL SERVICE

0   25   50

MILES

KEY TO CIRCLE SIZES
(PERSONS X 1000):

15   75   300   1,000

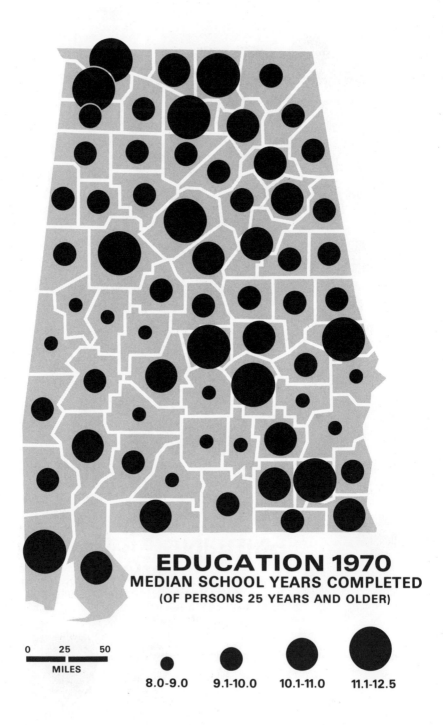

EDUCATION 1970
MEDIAN SCHOOL YEARS COMPLETED
(OF PERSONS 25 YEARS AND OLDER)

0   25   50
MILES

8.0-9.0   9.1-10.0   10.1-11.0   11.1-12.5

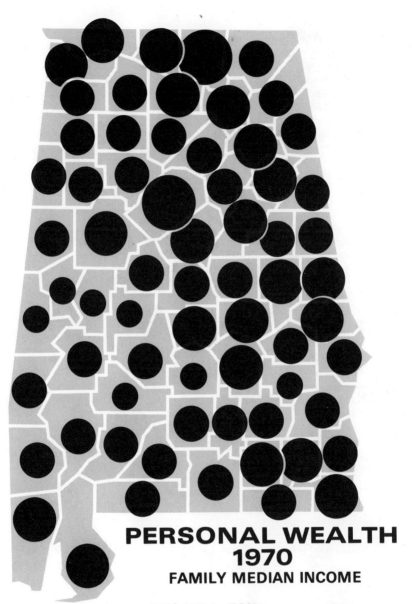

PERSONAL WEALTH
1970
FAMILY MEDIAN INCOME

DOLLARS (x 1000)

0   25   50
MILES

3.0-   4.6-   6.6-   8.6-
4.5   6.5   8.5   10.4

Alabama Authors

19th CENTURY

1.	Joseph G. Baldwin	1815-1864
2.	Elizabeth Bellamy	1837-1900
3.	Willis Brewer	1844-1912
4.	Jeremiah Clemens	1814-1865
5.	Zitella Cooke	c. 1840-1929
6.	Wiley Conner	c. 1795-1850?
7.	Kate Cumming	1835-1909
8.	J. L. M. Curry	1825-1903
9.	Thomas C. DeLeon	1839-1914
10.	John W. DuBose	1836-1918
11.	Joseph M. Field	1810-1856
12.	Peter J. Hamilton	1859-1927
13.	Caroline Hentz	1800-1856
14.	Henry W. Hilliard	1808-1892
15.	Johnson J. Hooper	1815-1862
16.	Francis B. Lloyd	1861-1897
17.	Noah M. Ludlow	1795-1886
18.	Alexander B. Meek	1814-1865
19.	Idora M. Moore	1843-1929
20.	Thomas M. Owen	1866-1920
21.	Samuel M. Peck	1854-1938
22.	Albert J. Pickett	1810-1858
23.	Anne Royall	1769-1854
24.	Father A. J. Ryan	1838-1886
25.	Raphael Semmes	1809-1877
26.	Sol. Smith	1801-1869
27.	William R. Smith	1815-1896
28.	Howard Weeden	1847-1905
29.	Augusta Evans Wilson	1835-1909
30.	John A. Wyeth	1845-1922

20th CENTURY

31.	Thomas P. Abernethy	1890-
32.	Richmond C. Beatty	1905-1961
33.	Jack Bethea	1892-1928
34.	Buford Boone	1909-
35.	Joe D. Brown	1915-
36.	James Saxon Childers	1899-1965
37.	Octavus Roy Cohen	1891-1959
38.	Lonnie Coleman	1920-
39.	Borden Deal	1922-
40.	Mary Fenollosa	1865-1954
41.	Walter L. Fleming	1874-1932
42.	Jesse Hill Ford	1928-
43.	Grover C. Hall	1888-1941
44.	William B. Huie	1910-
45.	Helen Keller	1880-1968
46.	Harper Lee	1926-
47.	William March	1894-1954
48.	Stephen L. Mooney	1915-
49.	John T. Moore	1858-1929
50.	Frank L. Owsley	1890-1956
51.	Julian L. Rayford	1908-
52.	Elise A. Sanguinetti	1926-
53.	T. S. Stribling	1881-1965
54.	Emma G. Sterne	1894-
55.	Hudson Strode	1893-
56.	Howell Vines	1899-
57.	Lella Warren	1899-
58.	Booker T. Washington	1856-1915
59.	Clement R. Wood	1888-1950
60.	Martha Young	1868-1941

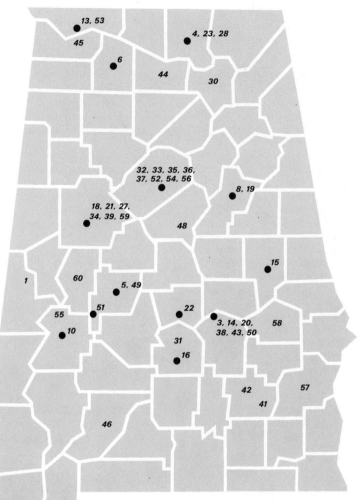

13, 53
45
6
4, 23, 28
44
30
32, 33, 35, 36,
37, 52, 54, 56
8, 19
18, 21, 27,
34, 39, 59
48
15
1
60
5, 49
55
51
22
3, 14, 20,
38, 43, 50
58
10
31
16
42
57
41
46
2, 7, 9, 11, 12,
17, 24, 25, 26,
29, 47, 51
40

ALABAMA AUTHORS

COMPILED BY
BENJAMIN B. WILLIAMS

0   25   50
MILES

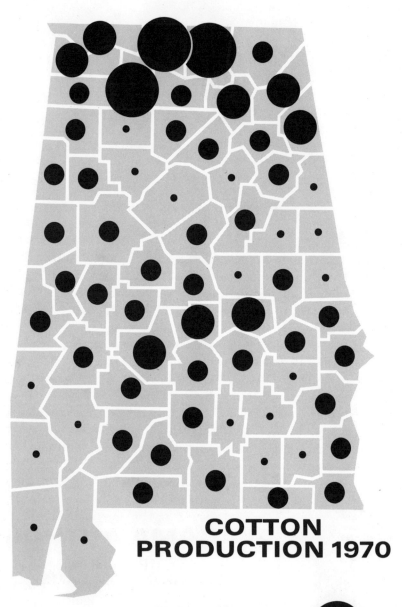

**COTTON
PRODUCTION 1970**

MILES

BALES (x 100)

1-20 21-135 136-250 251-634

Chapter Twelve

Alabama Trends 1860-1970

ALABAMA has experienced great growth in the past century in total population, urban population, transportation facilities, manufacturing developments, and the educational and financial resources of its residents. The state has also changed from a rural "Cotton State" to one with a diversified agriculture, extensive manufacturing, and a predominantly urban population. The decline in cotton production and the rural black population which traditionally supported it is a part of this change.

Although the total population has increased approximately 3½ times since 1860 (1 million to 3½ million), the black population has increased only twofold (437,770 to 903,467). Both the white and black populations are urban.

The distribution of Alabama's population has likewise undergone rapid change. In 1860, the Black Belt of South Alabama was the most densely populated area of the state; but by 1900 Birmingham's growth was apparent on population maps and by 1930 the "Magic City" had rival urban centers in Montgomery and Mobile. Although these two cities of South Alabama have retained a large number of residents, the North Alabama triangle of Tuscaloosa, Huntsville, and Gadsden-Anniston became the new population center of the state by 1970.

The black population showed a similar distribution during the 1860-1970 years. The 1860 and 1900 populations were centered in the Black Belt but the 1900 distribution was more urban with notable centers in Selma and Montgomery. The movement to the cities continued into 1930 and 1970 with Birmingham and Mobile also acquiring large numbers of black residents.

A large number of both white and black Alabamians became city dwellers during the past one-hundred years. The percent of the total

Alabama population which was urban increased from 5.1 in 1860 to 11.9 in 1900, 28.1 in 1930 (by which time the United States as a whole had become an urban nation, with more than one-half the residents living in cities larger than 2,500), and 58.4 percent in 1970.

The urban growth was paralleled by transportation system improvements and both were greatly influenced by the increase in manufacturing. The urbanized Alabama population was served by more transportation modes in 1970 than in 1860 with airports serving most major urban centers to supplement the 1900-1970 railroad development and the improvement of public roads following the automobile's invention. The key to many of these urban and transportation changes was manufacturing, particularly since World War II. Value added by manufacturing increased from $34,112,000 in 1899 to $258,125,000 in 1929 to $2,515,011,000 in 1963—approximately a tenfold increase in the last twenty-five years. The state distribution patterns of manufacturing were generally similar to that of urbanization, with the Black Belt and South and Central Alabama being superseded by Birmingham and Northeast Alabama as the chief manufacturing area of the state during the 1860-1970 years.

The urban, transportation, and manufacturing growth of Alabama has brought educational and financial benefits to the State's residents. The primitive public education system of the antebellum era has been replaced by a statewide system of public schools and colleges. The rate of illiteracy has also shown a steady decrease. Illiteracy continues heaviest in the Black Belt—an area with a continuing high percentage of black population (despite having decreasing *numbers* of blacks). The personal wealth of Alabamians increased greatly in the 1860-1970 period. Although more uniformly distributed statewide, the highest concentration of wealth shifted generally from the Black Belt to North Alabama.

The major area of decline in state productivity was cotton production. Cotton production had gradually increased from 989,955 bales in 1860 to 1,106,840 bales in 1900 and to a high of 1,312,963 bales in 1930 before declining to 507,000 bales in 1970. The intrastate distribution also changed from the Black Belt to the Tennessee Valley. Alabama no longer was a true "Cotton State" and the "Cotton Kingdom" had a new home.

In summary, Alabamians of the 1970s are more urban, more diversified in agriculture, more industrial, better educated, wealthier, and less reliant on the cotton crop than their 1860 counterparts. Developments since World War II suggest that these trends will continue.

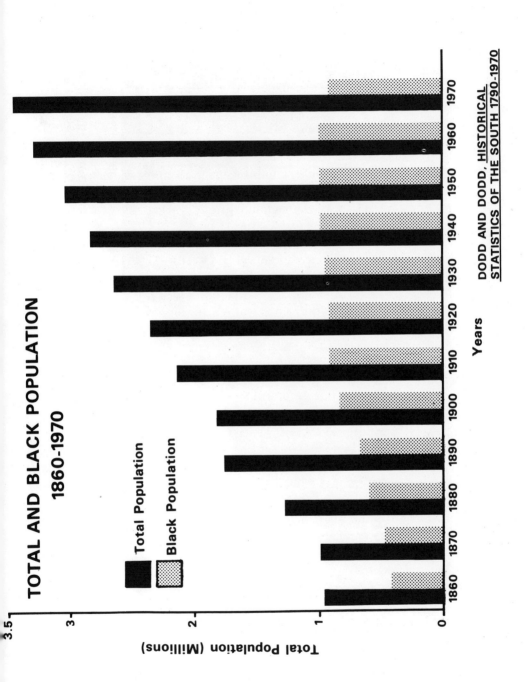

TOTAL AND BLACK POPULATION
1860-1970

Total Population

Black Population

Total Population (Millions)

Years

DODD AND DODD, HISTORICAL
STATISTICS OF THE SOUTH 1790-1970

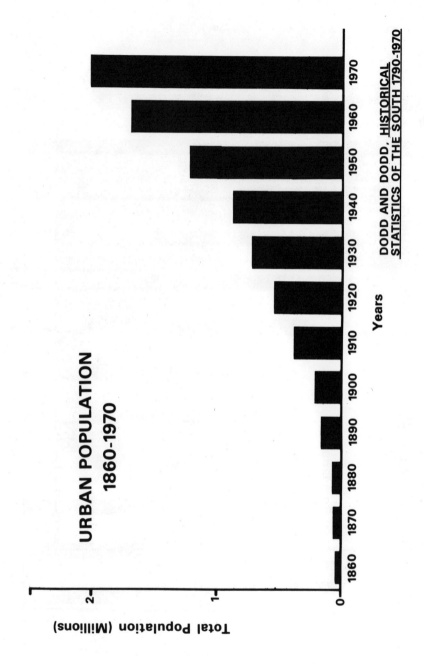

URBAN POPULATION
1860-1970

Total Population (Millions)

Years

DODD AND DODD, HISTORICAL
STATISTICS OF THE SOUTH 1790-1970

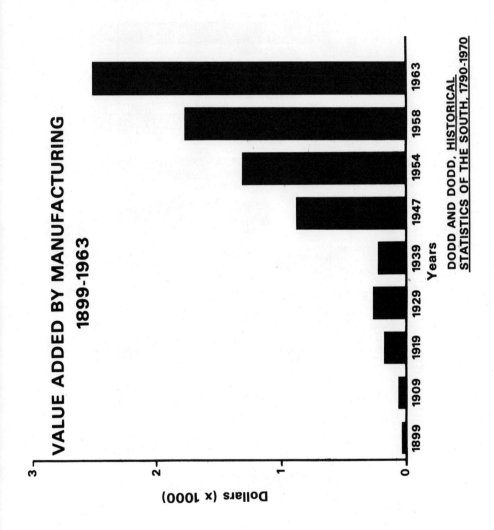

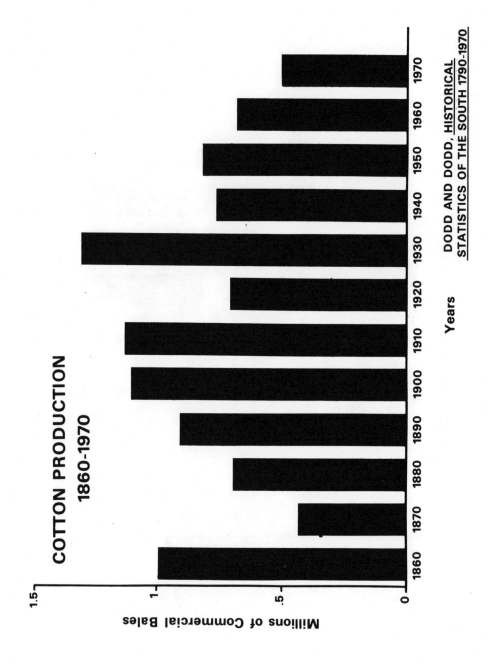

COTTON PRODUCTION
1860-1970

Millions of Commercial Bales

1.5

1

.5

0

1860 1870 1880 1890 1900 1910 1920 1930 1940 1950 1960 1970

Years

DODD AND DODD, HISTORICAL
STATISTICS OF THE SOUTH 1790-1970

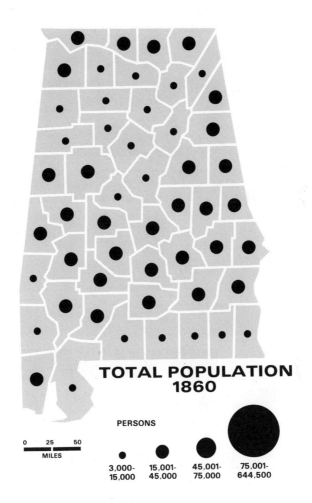

TOTAL POPULATION
1860

PERSONS

0   25   50
MILES

3,000-   15,001-   45,001-   75,001-
15,000   45,000   75,000   644,500

**TOTAL POPULATION
1900**

PERSONS

| 3,000-15,000 | 15,001-45,000 | 45,001-75,000 | 75,001-644,500 |

0   25   50
MILES

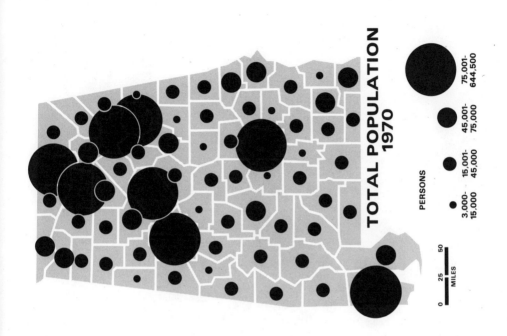

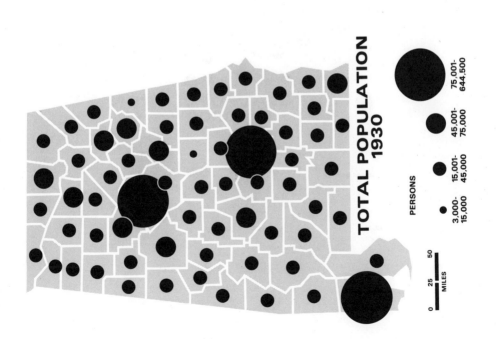

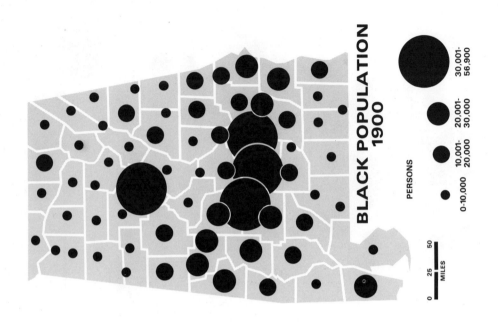

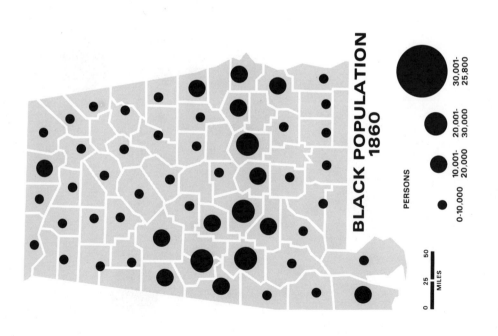

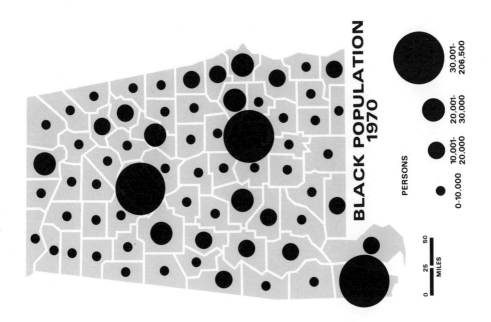

BLACK POPULATION
1930

PERSONS

0-10,000   10,001-   20,001-   30,001-
            20,000   30,000   168,000

0 25 50
MILES

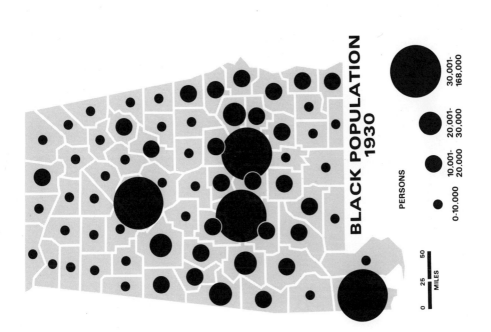

BLACK POPULATION
1970

PERSONS

0-10,000   10,001-   20,001-   30,001-
            20,000   30,000   206,500

0 25 50
MILES

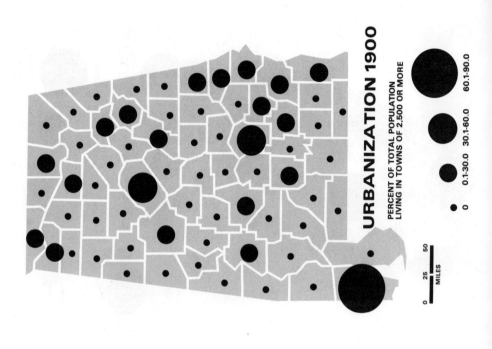

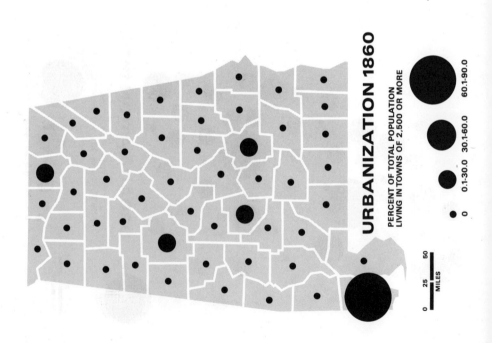

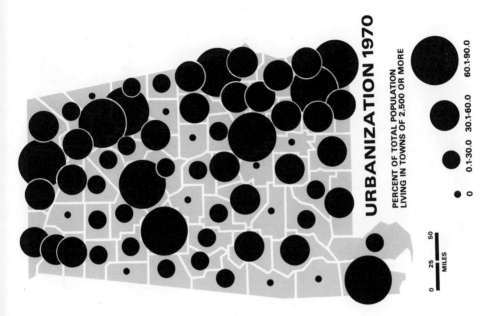

URBANIZATION 1970

PERCENT OF TOTAL POPULATION
LIVING IN TOWNS OF 2,500 OR MORE

60.1-90.0   30.1-60.0   0.1-30.0   0

0   25   50
MILES

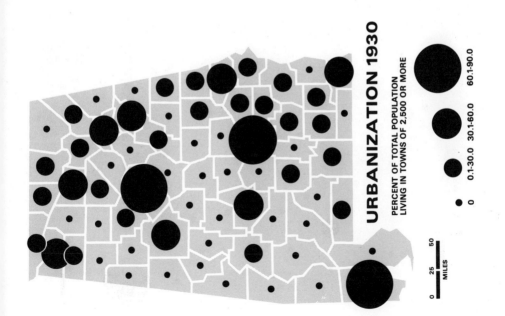

URBANIZATION 1930

PERCENT OF TOTAL POPULATION
LIVING IN TOWNS OF 2,500 OR MORE

60.1-90.0   30.1-60.0   0.1-30.0   0

0   25   50
MILES

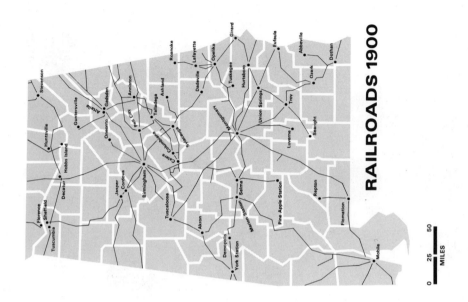

RAILROADS 1900

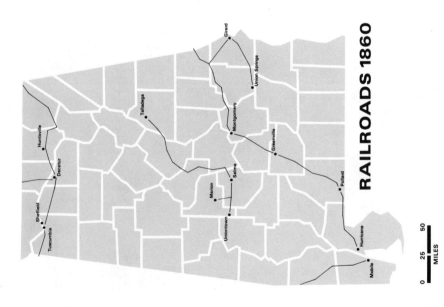

RAILROADS 1860

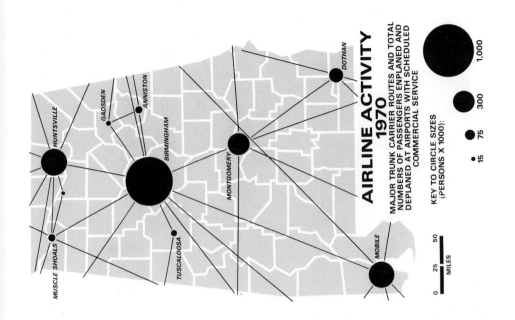

AIRLINE ACTIVITY 1970

MAJOR TRUNK CARRIER ROUTES AND TOTAL NUMBERS OF PASSENGERS ENPLANED AND DEPLANED AT AIRPORTS WITH SCHEDULED COMMERCIAL SERVICE

KEY TO CIRCLE SIZES (PERSONS X 1000):

1,000   300   75   15

0   25   50
MILES

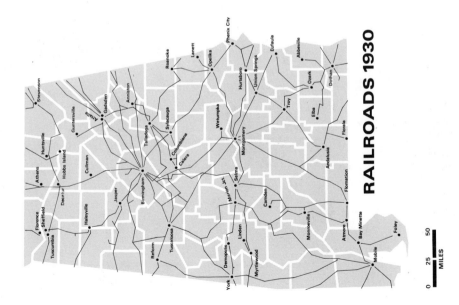

RAILROADS 1930

0   25   50
MILES

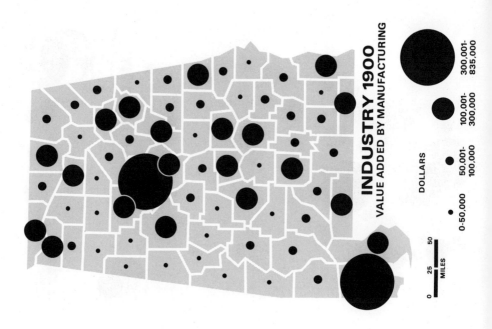

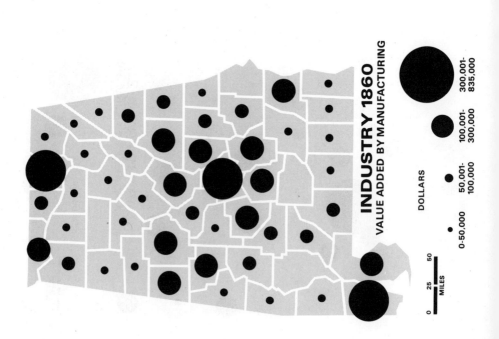

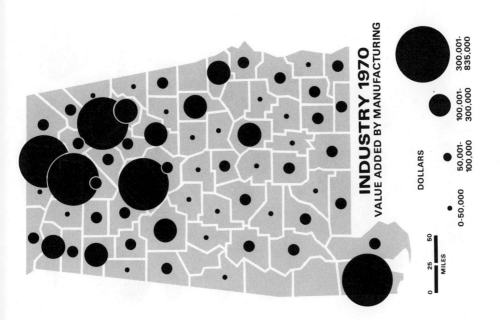

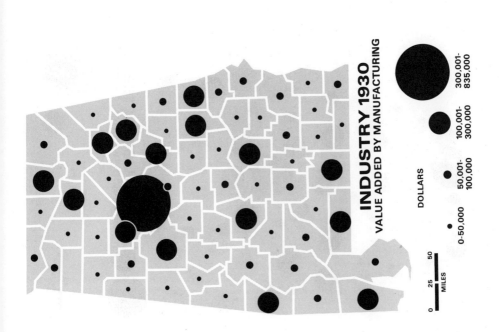

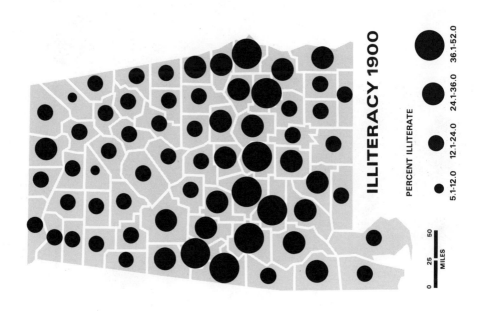

ILLITERACY 1900

PERCENT ILLITERATE

5.1-12.0   12.1-24.0   24.1-36.0   36.1-52.0

MILES
0   25   50

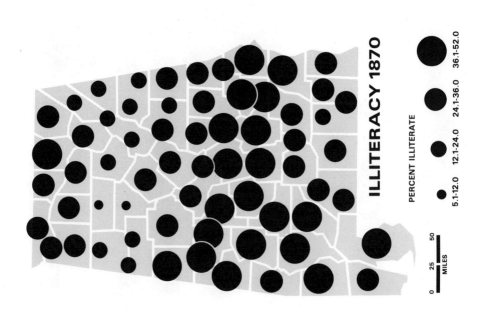

ILLITERACY 1870

PERCENT ILLITERATE

5.1-12.0   12.1-24.0   24.1-36.0   36.1-52.0

MILES
0   25   50

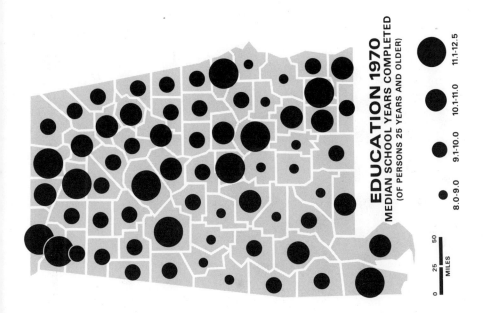

EDUCATION 1970
MEDIAN SCHOOL YEARS COMPLETED
(OF PERSONS 25 YEARS AND OLDER)

11.1-12.5   10.1-11.0   9.1-10.0   8.0-9.0

0 25 50
MILES

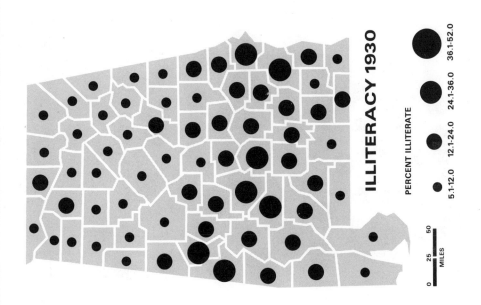

ILLITERACY 1930

PERCENT ILLITERATE

36.1-52.0   24.1-36.0   12.1-24.0   5.1-12.0

0 25 50
MILES

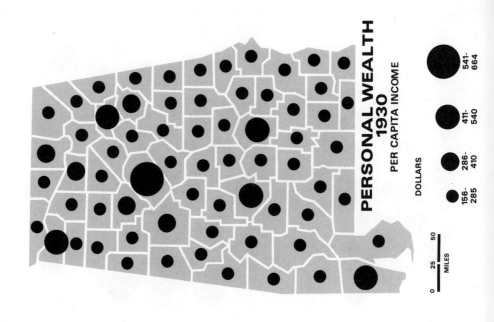

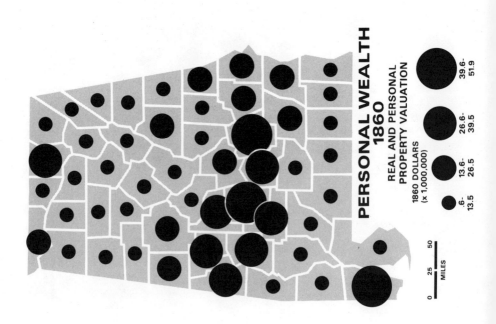

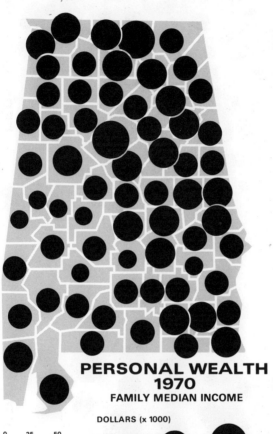

PERSONAL WEALTH
1970
FAMILY MEDIAN INCOME

DOLLARS (x 1000)

0   25   50
MILES

3.0-   4.6-   6.6-   8.6-
4.5   6.5   8.5   10.4

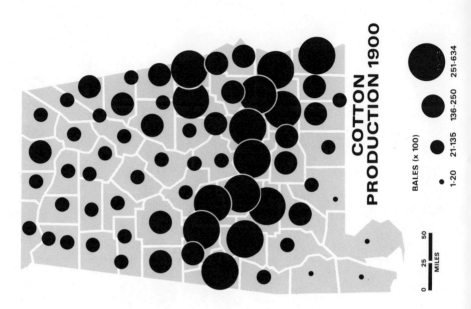

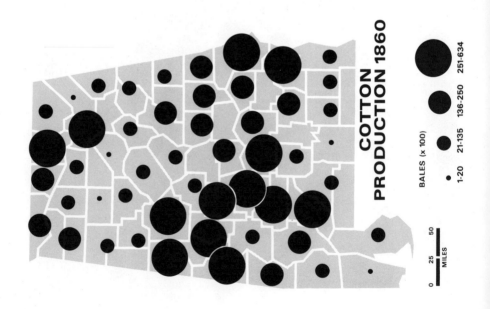

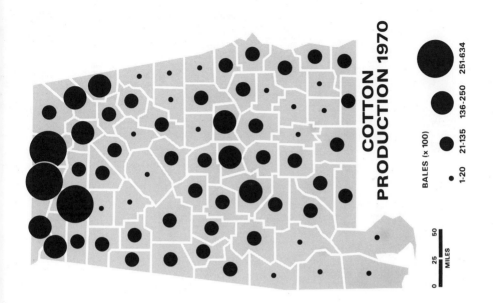

COTTON
PRODUCTION 1970

BALES (x 100)

1-20   21-135   136-250   251-634

0   25   50
MILES

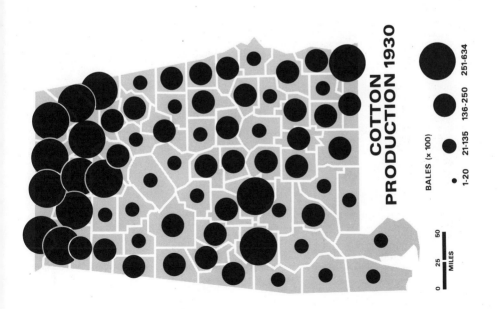

COTTON
PRODUCTION 1930

BALES (x 100)

1-20   21-135   136-250   251-634

0   25   50
MILES

Index